A WOMEN'S GATHERING DEVOTIONAL

TO ENCOURAGE, INSPIRE, AND GIVE HOPE
THROUGH MY OWN PERSONAL
EXPERIENCE IN LIFE

NIKKI ROSS

A WOMEN'S GATHERING DEVOTIONAL

Copyright © 2022 Nikki Ross

All rights reserved.

No part of this book may be reproduced, distributed or transmitted in any form by any means, graphic, electronic, or mechanical including photocopy, recording, taping or by any information storage or retrieval system, without permission in writing from the publisher, except in the case of reprints in the context of reviews, quotes or references.

Scripture quotations marked NLT are taken from the Holy Bible, New Living Translation Copyright © 1996, 2004, 2007, 2013, 2015 by Tyndale House Publishers Inc. Scripture quotations marked KJV are taken from the King James Version, Public domain. Scripture quotations marked MSG are taken from The Message Bible, Copyright © 1993, 1994, 1995, 1995, 1996, 2000, 2001, 2002 by Eugene H. Peterson. Scripture quotations taken from The Holy Bible, New International Version® NIV® Copyright © 1973, 1978, 1984, 2011 by Biblica, Inc.™

Used by permission. All rights reserved worldwide

Printed in the United States of America

ISBN: 979-8-9868570-0-8

Dedication

To my 3 k's: Kanesha, Kaz'jah and K'la. Your Momma did it again, flaws and all. I am super proud to have overcome so many obstacles in my life and you girls have witnessed some of my hurdles. I thank God for His powers in all He has allowed me to witness and endure because that means that I'm still here another day to get things right in my life and yours. Just know I couldn't do anything I do without you girls. I love you and I truly thank God for each of you.

Kanesha, I pray a fresh wind over *KNR Interior Designs*. May every thought and great idea of yours come to life. No event will ever be too big or small for your business. Keep believing, and fear not for you are with Thee (God). I pray that you always remember where your help comes from. It's the Lord and you know He'll make a way for you out of no way. Anything that you want and need, just ask in His name. ANYTHING.

Kazjah, *Bratz Doll House* will be a household name if you put your best foot forward. Kaz'jah, everything that you touch comes to life. Continue being consistent in your fashion and beauty world. You can have every woman calling on you for face beats by KY. God blessed you to be bold, creative and a leader. Embrace your gifts and you'll go places far beyond the limits of where money can take you.

K'la Ross, my third child. My #3 in the WNBA. Keep your mind focused and the world will know your name like you said at 4 years old. Keep your head in those books.

Remain positive and productive and your circle small. You can have everything you want if you just believe.

I pray that God will keep his hands upon you all and I pray no weapons formed against you three girls shall prosper in Jesus's Holy name.

Amen.

Contents

Introduction 1
Day 1: Healing 4
Day 2: Miracles, Signs, and Wonders 6
Day 3: Addiction 9
Day 4: Weapons 12
Day 5: Why Worry 14
Day 6: The Cycles 16
Day 7: Dropping A Jewel 18
Day 8: You're stronger than you Know 20
Day 9: The Dead End 22
Day 10: The Vision 24
Day 11: Let it Go 26
Day 12: Thankful 28
Day 13: God's Word is Everlasting 30
Day 14: The Still Moment 33
Day 15: Identify Yourself 35
Day 16: Temptation 37
Day 17: The Overcomer 40
Day 18: Confirmation 42
Day 19: Just Imagine 44
Day 20: The Way God Do Thangs 47
Day 21: Let's Praise God 49
Day 22: Ground Zero 51

Day 22: Testing, Testing 54
Day 23: The Good 56
Day 24: Dropping a Jewel: Being Determined 58
Day 25: My Strength 60
Day 26: The Abandonment.. 62
Day 27: A Mouth Full.. 66
Day 28: Pain and suffering in its PURPOSE 68
Day 29: Get out of God's Way 70
Day 29: "Trust Him"...72
Day 30: God first... 74
Day 31: Intentional 76
Day 32: You are the Light 79
Day 33: The Crown 81
Day 34: Tempted 84
Day 35: "Faith".. 87
Day 36: Wherever You Are, God is...................................... 89
Day 37: The FIGHT 91
Day 38: The Fight Continues (Repeat Offender)............... 93
Day 39: VIOLATION 96
Day 39: Dropping a Jewel 99
Day 40: The Boat (Noah's Ark) 101
Day 41: I Will Make You Hunger so When I bless, You'll be Humble...104
January 30,2022...107

Introduction

The Women's Gathering

Everything that I've placed in this book is either because I've experienced it or My Father in Heaven has placed it on my heart to write about it. I am a firm believer that our experiences as human beings are similar. God created us in His image so that is explainable. To help me fully understand my life walk and all that it entails, I studied the Bible, applied my experiences and reflected. Initially, understanding the Bible was difficult. Don't get it twisted, I am under some awesome leadership. My pastor is the best and provides me with messages and classes to help me walk right. I realized that I needed to know the scriptures for myself. I needed to be able to connect with God in my own way through His word. As I am writing this Women's Devotional, I am starting to gain an even greater understanding of who He is and who He is not. The Women's Gathering devotional has helped me and I believe that as you travel along with me, it will help you too.

Why a "Women's Gathering"? I am so glad that you asked.

In 2019, I wanted to form a women's group. This group would consist of women with similar life experiences who were willing to encourage, inspire and give hope to other women. After God, another woman can help to heal another woman. I believe that is a part of our legacy on this earth. When women come together and freely share, lives are changed. This was my heart's desire in 2019. I can remember our first outing. Eight women met in my backyard that day and discussed relationships and love. That experience was so powerful that it prompted me to host the second gathering the next year. In 2020, I hosted the 2nd Women's Gathering at Thirst Restaurant and Lounge. This gathering was called the BGX Luncheon in honor of my first book "The Blac Girl Experience". 12 bold and beautiful women attended this event. They held nothing back. It was after this gathering that I understood the importance of me continuing to provide spaces for women to connect. Mindsets were shifted. At that event, a young lady who previously worked with me admitted that she wasn't fond of me initially, all because of the opinions of others. It would take this event for her to truly understand who I was. That's the beauty of connection. That's the power of authenticity and transparency. That's the goal of the Women's gathering.

In 2021, the "Wow Moment" Luncheon was born. 20 women participated and when I say that the name manifested itself, it manifested itself. There were "wow" moments and testimonies galore. From the very beginning, God "wowed" me. My Cousin, Zena Thompson came down from Greenville, North Carolina to tell her testimony. That testimony set Tasha, a good girlfriend of mine, free. She was freed from the dark place of grief from the loss of her husband of over 25 years of marriage. My friend had lost all hope and didn't know how she was going to go on. After Zena shared her testimony of losing every life that was in her house, the shackles on Tasha were released. I couldn't have made this up if I tried. God connected the dots. I was just obedient enough to follow God's plans. I didn't know that by planning this Women's Gathering that it would do all that it had done. I envisioned it to be one thing and God ordained it to be "More than Enough". It became a movement. A safe place for women to be set free. A judge free zone. A gathering place for every woman hurt or healed. The women's gathering became a place for women needing reassurance.

One of my proudest moments was at The Women's Gathering: The Purpose Event. This event seated 125 women dressed in all Black. Unity was all in the room. It was powerful to witness. The atmosphere was filled with expectation, hope and God's presence. The Word of Encouragement Cards were on point. Each card that the ladies received was the one that they needed. When I wrote out those cards, I asked God to please show himself mighty and speak to every woman's current situation. He did just that. We laughed, cried, prayed and embraced every moment together as God would have it. Again, that's the power of the "Women's Gathering."

I hope and pray this WGE Devotional inspires someone to be set free from any hurt or trauma they may have endured in life. I pray that it sets fire to someone who wants to tell their truth. I pray this Devotional will get in the hands of every person in need of it. I pray that this Devotional will sell out all over the world and that there will be more to come for me and every woman attached to it. For every woman who will read this Devotional, I pray for healing and deliverance over your mind, body and spirit and that you will allow God into your hearts.

Day 1

Healing

Psalm 147:3 "He heals the Brokenhearted and binds up their wounds."

Hearing that God has the power to clear up wounds and mend our broken hearts is beyond blessed. I've seen Him clean me up so many times. Thank you Lord for all you've done for me.

Healing must be how we start this Women's Gathering Devotional. Let's pray.

Heavenly Father, I'm coming to You as humble as I know how to send a prayer up for healing. Father God, You are our source of healing. In you, we find everything we need. We know you will supply us with it all. Fill us up with your healing powers so that we may be whole again, Jesus. There is nothing we can't do without You, Lord. So, have Your way in my situation. Have Your way in the person reading this prayer. There is nothing too hard for You. Every broken thing can be fixed through You, Father. Again have Your way in us today and the days to come.

Healing is more than money to me, Lord and I pray the world gets healed so that there will be love and peace on earth. I pray for healing for my husband, children, family and friends. In Jesus's Holy name I pray. Amen.

So many of us repeatedly fail in our marriages, relationships and even friendships because we hold on to unresolved trauma. Those wounds that we endure can't be healed because we won't seek help. We won't seek God or we don't think anything is wrong. We become content with the way things are. We may be in denial about the things we've been through in life. Healing is a process of becoming healthy again. Healing occurs through the integrating voices that restore, transform and nurture the whole person's mind, body and spirit. Our minds become sharper when we heal. Our body becomes lighter in what we carry through healing. Our spirits become lifted when we heal.

I can help others through situations even while I'm healing. People say that it is not possible but I beg to differ. Even in my brokenness, I have been able to help someone else. They didn't even know what was going on with me until I revealed it at the end of the phone conversation. That's just the way God works. When I operated in obedience, I too was set free. When God downloads in me and I'm thinking I'm encouraging someone, I'm getting encouraged. Think about the times that you have been able to be a blessing to someone during your own healing process. When you are truly healed, you can speak from a place of love and wisdom fully. The healing process is continuous. Pay attention to your triggers and let them lead you to a place of healing instead of hurt. May this day be blessed.

Day 2

Miracles, Signs, and Wonders

Amos 9:13-15 MSG

"Yes, indeed it won't be long now. God decreed things are going to happen so fast your head will swim. One thing, fast, on the heels of the other. You won't be able to keep up. Everything will be happening at once and everywhere you look blessings! Blessings like wine pouring off the mountains and hills. I will make everything right again for my people in Israel. They'll rebuild their ruined cities. They'll plant vineyards and drink good wine. They'll work their gardens and eat fresh vegetables and I'll plant them, plant them on their own land. They will never again be uprooted from the land I've given them. God, your God, says so."

I received this scripture from a pastor/ friend named Marvin Green. He spoke this scripture over my life during my 1st book deal. The funny thing was he had no clue that I was in the process of writing an Everyday Devotional for Women. God had already ordered my steps to write this Devotional. I know He had the assignment for me and I was given several confirmations to focus on this solely. As I was in the editing stages of the Blac Girl Experience book, my editor, Alicia Hill Jones corrected probably my entire book but I noticed there weren't any corrections needed when I started writing little devotional notes in the back of the Blac

Girl Experience book. I was shocked to see how she just corrected that whole book yet didn't have corrections on any of the stuff talking about God. That's when I knew that writing about my experience and God's guidance through it was what I was supposed to be writing.

It's nothing like going through something when you have God on your side. It is hard going through life not knowing God. Your choices may not always be wise. Wrong decisions could be damaging when there's no God. The path you chose to take could lead you down a road of destruction. When God is in it, victory is won. God becomes your source and your guidance. You'll begin to seek Him for everything. When I turned my focus to Him, I instantly started seeing Him moving on my behalf. Things were happening just like the scripture read. I would be praying about things and throughout the day what I prayed for happened right before my eyes. I'm talking about my 2022 year. God's presence started becoming more visible to me. The Holy Spirit would remind me of the things of God every time my prayers were answered. That was a reminder to give God praise. That's the way I looked at it. Yes, I'm standing on this scripture Amos 13-15. God promised me these things so I must stand on it and watch it all come into my life. You must believe, have faith, pray and trust God. #TheGodlyGirl

💡 Thought for Today:

God will send you help when you're in need. Call out for it. Believe in your heart it can be done. During this season of my life, God has sent so many signs of His presence my way. There were times when I still didn't catch on that it was Him with me. God started showing me Him in real time. I started to understand the realness of His presence. He began to heal the things that were hurting me. When I was drowning, He became my rescuer. I learned how to call on Him. If you say nothing, you will see nothing. Remember, a closed mouth doesn't get fed. Learn to communicate with your Heavenly Father. What you went through is for you to experience and overcome. God wants to use you to be a witness for His namesake. Go through life so you can be that vessel someone needs.

♫ **Song for Today: Forever is a Long Time by Jason Nelson**

Day 3

Addiction

1 Corinthians 10:13 "No test or temptation that comes your way is beyond the course of what others have had to face. All you need to remember is that God will never let you down; He'll never let you be pushed past your limits; He will always be there to help you come through it."

This "inspired experience" came while I was on a great roll of success. I had written my first book, The Blac Girl Experience. Book sales were good. I was even having a few speaking engagements but I became distracted. So distracted to the point I was spending money like crazy. I began spending time doing things that were taking my money. It got so bad that I didn't have any money to save. One Friday, I ended up losing everything. I remember taking a gamble and thinking I would win more money. I had never been a gambler before but I thought because I was this good person, always there for everyone else, doing right in life, I thought I would win.

Yes, that's the sick game your mind plays on you when you're in an addiction. I had gotten so caught up, I was losing everything. I was losing sight of myself and my fresh walk with God. To make matters worse, only me and God knew what was really going on. It was bad. I had never had something to have a hold on me like this gambling addiction. This continued for 2 years. Throughout this process, I had choices to do what's right or keep inflicting these wounds on myself.

I asked God "why are you allowing me to be this foolish? Why haven't you intervened." The Holy Spirit spoke and said "you have a choice in this matter to do it or not. What you're doing you know it's not right and you choose to take a gamble with your money. You must learn this lesson on your own. if you choose me, God, victory is mine, said the Lord." There is nothing to lack in the Lord. My finances may have been low but I knew God would always provide. That's what I had to tell myself. That day, I decided to choose the right way, God's way, after losing my money. God showed up instantly. I began receiving orders for my book right in the parking lot of the casino. I sold more copies than usual of my book sales. That's when I knew it was time to get back on course and I was obedient. God began to give me what I needed to put this devotional together.

All of my experiences, the good and bad ones, had to be shared. Someone needs to hear it. Someone going through the same addiction may need a way out of it. I became so determined to share my truth, that I started Googling the word "distractions". In the Bible and it was over 25 scriptures that came up for what I had just been dealing with that was distracting me. A distraction is when you are dragged away from your task and that was exactly what had happened to me. The enemy dragged me good. Did it happen so I could learn from it? Did it happen so I could share it? Maybe but Satan has a way of taking you off course when he knows the blessings in your life. Satan has no new tricks but what he does have is knowledge of your weakness. He will use them to throw you off course. I just know God has never taken His hands off me No matter where I have been in my life. Regardless of my circumstances, He has never left my side, only correcting me with His love. Whenever I cried out to him, I could always count on the Holy Spirit to answer me.

If you don't stay on course, you'll never make it to your destination of success. I had to give myself a pep talk back then. I would say to myself "you want to speak to many women across the world. You want to encourage others. You want to walk in your purpose of giving hope to those that lack, right? Well, stay on course. You can't encourage anyone if you don't finish the task at hand." That's what the Holy Spirit was saying to me as I started writing again. Yes, you will get off course but start over again and don't stop until you finish.

☀ Thought for Today:

In life, you will find times when you must push the reset button. Turn everything off and hit reset. Then, inhale, exhale and breathe. This time when you begin again, everything old will be erased and rebooted to the new "YOU". #TheGodlygirl

♫ Song of the Day: LOVE by God's Property

Day 4

Weapons

Isaiah 54:17 "But No weapon that can hurt you has ever been forged. Any accuser who takes you to court will be dismissed as a liar. This is what God's servant can expect. I'll see to it that everything works out for the best. God's Decree."

When I tell you that everything that you may go through in life is already written. Nothing has ever happened in your life that hasn't happened in the Bible. For many years, I would hear this scripture from older family members and even some young. No weapons formed against me shall prosper. It's one thing to hear it. it's something else to see happen right before your eyes. Many of my life experiences are shareable moments. For example, I had just received a text message stating that I was about to lose something so precious to me. At first, I wanted to react to the situation because I don't take threats lightly. As I continued reading the text message, the angrier I became. The flesh will rise during an emotional state quickly. But the Holy Spirit came to the rescue yet again. For every bad, there's a good. For every dark time, there is light. I heard that sweet sound in my ear speak so clearly. "Don't you dare get weary in well-doing. God will fight your battles and win. Lean not on your own understanding but in all your ways acknowledge Him and He'll quickly make your path straight."

It wasn't until that moment that I finally understood. You must get in the word and stand on the word to get through the bumps in the road. Invite God into your situation. Everybody doesn't know the God you serve. When the enemy comes into your space, pray until it flees. All I could come up with was this prayer **Isaiah 54:17 No weapon formed against me share prosper.** I kept saying not knowing that things were working for me. I asked God to turn that situation around for me. You can have all the money in the world but nothing can go against God. I know firsthand that the weapons will try and form but won't prosper. Sit back and allow God to do the rest. First, you must believe that God will do what He said He would do. He will stand by His word. He'll fight your every battle. He'll turn your dark nights into days. He'll bless you even in a mess. He'll make a way for you that you didn't even see coming. That's why you must pray daily, believe and keep the faith. Sometimes, we forget who really has our back. Just look to the sky and know that nobody does it like the Lord. I will leave you with this piece. All that you put in your family, friends and love, put it in God and see what He'll do for you.

💡 Thought for Today:

Everything that YOU will experience in Life, YOU will Overcome. #TheGodlyGirl

🎵 Song For Today: NO WEAPONS by Fred Hammond

Day 5

Why Worry

Psalms 27 (KJV) "The Lord is my light and salvation, whom shall I fear? The Lord is the strength of my life, whom shall I be afraid? When the wicked, even my enemies, and my foes, came upon me to eat up my flesh, they stumbled and fell.

I had to know what Psalms 27 was really talking about. Psalms 27 is a cry for help.Ultimately, it is a declaration of belief in the greatness of God and trust in the protection God provides. Why do we get so worried or worked up with things when they don't go our way? Why do we even ask the question "why" when God already knows the answer? Especially, when we know God has already figured it out. There is a purpose for everything. Some of our experiences are lessons. Oftentimes, these things happen to me and I would get so worked up about it. This morning, I choose to wake up and declare that the battle is the Lord's. It may be assigned to me but I can confidently put it in God's hands. When fear tries to take over because we aren't in control or uncomfortable, we must realize that it is the work of the "flesh man". Our flesh sows doubt. Our spirit reveals the truth. The truth is found in God's word. Fear Not, God is with us. Psalms 27 is strong and mighty enough to stand on. My thoughts for today:

☀ Thought for Today:

Our minds are blessed to be able to remember, memorize bad thoughts and experiences in life. The mind is powerful enough to store it within. We must be careful of the things we allow our minds to absorb. Our minds build things so know it is truly a blessing to be in your right mind. Keep it filled with positivity and good thoughts. Remember to always allow God to activate the powers of the mind.

♪ Song of the day: Better With You In It by Major

Day 6

The Cycles

Romans 8:1(NIV) "Therefore, there is now no condemnation for those who are in Christ Jesus because through Christ Jesus, the law of the spirit who gives life has set you free from the laws of sin and death. For what the law was powerless to do because it was weakened by the flesh, God did by sending His own son in the likeness of sinful flesh to be a sin offering. And so, He condemned sin in the flesh in order that the righteous requirement of the law might be fully met in us, who do not live according to the flesh but according to the spirit."

This Bible verse spoke to me immediately. At this very moment, it fits like a glove. I keep running to this thing that is making me totally powerless. It's only taking away from me and my household. Have you ever felt like because you're the good person, the one who treats everybody right, you prayed day and night and everything supposed to happen that you want to happen in your life? I'm the first to tell you it doesn't work that way. Everything works according to God's plan not ours. The flesh believes everything is supposed to come right then and there. Now, I'm not saying you can't speak things into existence, because you can. Just don't think your life won't be overpowered by those of the flesh. God's plan for your life is what's best for you.

Lately, I have been traveling down the wrong road, going through stop signs without looking both ways. That's the flesh part of me. I was trying to rush the process only to look and see everything I was working towards is now a little delayed because of my flesh. I didn't want to see it through my Father in Heaven's eyes but through my own. You cannot get anywhere without the help of the Lord. He has you when no one else does. He'll give you the desires of your heart. Just trust the process. It is best for you.

☀ My Thought For Today:

Sometimes in life you may have to repeat a cycle or learning experience. Why? Because you didn't learn the 1st time. As you become wiser in the words, you'll elevate and not repeat.

♫ Song of the day: Just like God by Evvie McKinney

Day 7

Dropping A Jewel

> *Fear: An unpleasant emotion caused by being aware of danger; a feeling of being afraid. A feeling of respect and wonder for something very powerful.*

> *Faith: Complete trust or confidence in someone or something. Strong belief in God or in the Doctrine of a Religion based on Spiritual Apprehension.*

I've been in both places and it doesn't feel good to fear anything. It's impossible to get far in life thriving off fear. Fear can stop you from accomplishing a lot. Fear can stop your vision, your thought process and your progress. It can even stop you from believing in yourself. Right now, as I'm typing this message, I must be honest with you because I'm honest with myself (sometimes a little too honest). I'm in a situation right now that I'm a little fearful of the outcome. I don't know what in the world to do. I want to call my Momma, my daughter, my cousins and even my best friends but the Holy Spirit says "call on the Lord". I did but He didn't respond fast enough. And yes, I know God's timing is perfect. I know that if you don't invite God into your troubles, confusion will kick in, doubt consumes you and that known activation of fear invites himself in too. Yet again, here comes the Holy Spirit saying "call on the Lord".

That's the part that I do love about my relationship with God. He'll never leave nor forsaken me. The Holy Spirit gives me the comfort and constant reminder of the Lord's words and promises. Then, the scripture comes into play. "Weeping may endure for night but joy comes in the morning". Meaning, I may be crying today but tomorrow will be a new day filled with joy, peace and happiness. The only way to understand that is to apply faith and listen for the Holy Spirit. God has a marvelous way of doing things. He'll give you signs of comfort through people, places or things. As I was having a moment, I looked down at my phone to see a text message from a friend of mine who sends me daily affirmations or positive messages. This one was it. It read "Good morning. Nothing is permanent. So, don't stress yourself too much because no matter how bad the situation seems know it will change". I immediately went into praising God in the shower, crying out to Him because I needed him and He came right on time. My second confirmation came after walking through the beauty salon. My stylist, Dana says to me soon as I walked through the door, "I love you,Nikki." It was as if God was assuring me of His love. She continued telling me about the good things that I do in life and how I impact others. It was God speaking to me through her. I quickly came to realize that I can do nothing in fear but everything through faith. That's why it's good to have a relationship with God and know the word of God. You need to have something to stand on in a fearful moment. The key to overcome is to know this scripture. **"Lean not on your own understanding but in all your ways acknowledge Him and He will make your path straight." Proverbs 3:5-6**

Day 8

You're stronger than you Know.

Deuteronomy 31: 6 "Be strong and courageous. Do not be afraid or terrified because of them, for the Lord your God goes with you. He will never leave nor forsake you."

Everyday has a different lesson to learn. What today has taught me is that you must lean on God no matter what it looks like or how it feels. When you get in a situation that seems to be too much or intimidating, rely on the good book: the Bible. It's the best guideline to go by. I had an experience that shook my faith to the point where I didn't think to look for my refuge in Jesus Christ. It made me panic which means I wasn't relying on my faith but relying on my flesh. That can be a bit confusing and scary if allowed. I knew all I had to do was open the Bible but because we are human, it doesn't always happen that way. God uses signs of all sorts to give us a word of comfort or encouragement. This time, He used my sister in Christ, Pastor Shantelle Jefferson to send me a word. The word she sent was what I needed at the time. It was confirmation of what I was going through. No, she didn't know of my situation, but I know it was only God sending her to give me the word of encouragement. That's just what God does. He'll come right on time to give you strength when you're weak. He'll give you healing when you're hurt. He'll give you peace that will surpass all understanding. He'll give directions when you become lost. That's the God we serve. You must get to know Him to understand that.

When I felt my situation was becoming too much, I started thinking of different ways to win. As I reflect, I must laugh. See you can go to a fight not even sure if you're going to win or not, but when you allow God to fight your battles, victory is already won. All of that overthinking, restless nights and weary thoughts. All of it was unnecessary. "Rest easy, my child is what I heard. I did it once and I'll do it again. It's nothing too hard for Me. I've fought all your battles and won even the ones you didn't know about. Remember in order to win you have to put it in My hands and leave it there."

Have your way, Lord. Give me strength, courage and wisdom to use along this day. I know, no weapons formed against me or anyone attached to me on this day shall prosper, Cover those reading this message right now. Whatever they stand in need of, supply them, Lord.

Know God is the battle fighter. Turn it over to Him. His "Win" is guaranteed.

☀ My Thought for Today:

When you Know God, you have to trust God. I mean fully trust Him. Cast your cares to Him. Give your battles to Him and He'll supply all your needs.

♪ Song of the Day: Trouble Don't Last Always by Rev Timothy Wright

Day 9

The Dead End

The word "Dead" can be described in several ways. No longer alive, which is absent from the body is to be present with the Lord. Deprived of life, no more, expired, departed or gone. When something is dead it no longer exists. There's no bringing something dead back to life. Only God can do that. Dead doesn't just mean death. Sometimes some situations and relationships can also be considered dead. I've come to realize that everything has an expiration date. Sometimes, we try our best to bring life to a dead situation. Just speaking from my own experience. In life, you cannot water something that can no longer grow, that is no longer good for you or even things that can't help you to be a better you. I'm not speaking of a dead person but things that are considered dead weight in your life.

Dead weight can be family, friendships, relationships, coworkers etc. We must know that when there's no more life in it, it's time to put an end to it. It has taken many mistakes, heartaches and wrong decisions before I realized something was finished. I'm not sure why it took me so long to realize dead situations have expired. I just always want to see the good in everything and everybody. Some people can figure it out at the first sign of things not going right. In my case, I want to always breathe life in the dead stuff. When I do this I only end up hurting or disappointing myself. So much time is wasted trying to revive something dead. Time that I could be spending nurturing myself or just embracing what life has to offer me. After my last dead-end situation, I promised myself that I would spend more time getting "me" right. The time I wasted trying to be more for others I could've been further in life. I know everything happens the way it is supposed to happen though. If I had not gone through those dead-end situations, I would never know what the end of something looks like.

☼ Thought for today:

Remember you will only repeat things if you don't learn from them the first time. Dead ends have no place to go.

♫ Song of the Day: Do it Lord by Benjamin Dube ft. Jekalyn Carr

Day 10

The Vision

Habakkuk 2:2 "And the Lord answered me, and said," Write the vision, and make it plain upon tables that he may run that read it."

Writing the vision down for me is a normal thing. The things that I wrote and believed in were coming to life like the Scripture said. God's promise is His promise. We must stand strong on His word. Today, I know better. It's good to write everything down for God to see your Vision. Whether you want it in or out of your life. Write it down for your good. Trust me, I wrote my entire business plan out to a tee on a composition notebook and it came to life just like I wrote it. From the way you enter the door to the structure of the building, it was just like I had it in the book. When you write the vision, you must write it out from beginning to end. Who do you want to be a part of it? How much do you want to make? Who do you want to come? Be very detailed. From the bricks to the flooring, write it down. Pray about it. Believe in it. Sow into it and watch it manifest into the universe just as you would have it. God has a way about blessing us but we must do our part. Your faith activates what you believe and the things that you dream. Even though God has the Master plan, it's written in the Bible for us to believe. I'm a living witness to what God can do. He has done it for me so

I'm passing it on to you. Write it down and God will surely do the rest.

☀ Thought for Today:

Your prayers keep you connected to God. Don't ever stop praying. Don't ever stop believing. Everything is on God's time. His timing is perfect.

♬ Song of the Day: God's Got a blessing by Norman Hutchins

Day 11

Let it Go

Not sure why I didn't have a lot to say about the topic "Letting Go" because there's a lot of things I had to let go. I had to release family, being the go-to person, Johnny on the spot, always being available for people that would disappear at the sight of my call or presence. I had to let go of abandonment issues, grudges and putting myself last to make others happy first. This is a continuous process. There's still more things to release. I owe all my experiences for these stories or words of encouragement. It's no coincidence why I wrote this because God has given me every title, every experience to write all this stuff in this Devotional. From the things I've overcome, even to the things that may seem a bit challenging or impossible to defeat.

It's the hand of God upon me that I'm able to live through my life experiences and freely talk about it. It's something about letting go. I keep repeating this experience in life. When I tell you it comes in every season of my life just in different ways. Look at Day 7: You're Stronger Than You Know or Day 9: The End. I just keep revisiting this one tough cookie of a lesson. After many disappointments, I've finally learned that the reason you keep repeating is simply because you haven't learned from what you experienced. This also happens when you allow your heart to lead. Your heart can take you down the wrong road. It's just like being in school. You take a course and if you don't know the work, you fail. What do you do when you fail at something? You must repeat.

I'm learning something at this very moment. Even though you repeat a lesson, there is something new that you must gain in the repeated course. This time, I gained wisdom, something I didn't get the first time I experienced trying to let some things go. Wisdom for me is having the knowledge to know better and do better. If I would've gotten it the first time, I'm sure I wouldn't have had to repeat it. In everything that you do, use wisdom. Don't rush through your test in life. Everything has a process. Using wisdom will help you get it right the first time.

💡 Thought for today:

Change the things you can change and pray about the things you can't. Father God in heaven, I pray that everything that I have experienced in life doesn't have to be repeated. Unless it is me sharing what I went through to help someone else. Not taking anything from my learning experiences today but I want to see more of life and more of Your goodness. I want to see more blessings, more testimony, and all things good. More unity, more relationship with You. I want more of you, God. Amen

🎵 Song of the day: Endow Me by Coko

Day 12

Thankful

The Bible says "Give thanks in all circumstances". 1Thessalonians 5:16. God's word also teaches us to rejoice in the Lord always.

You don't just wake up every morning in a thankful mode. Well, at least it doesn't happen that way for me. I am not saying that I'm not thankful. Some days are better than others. When things look hopeless in our lives while going through life experiences, we sometimes need a little help turning our situations around. Doing that can come in many ways such as being around good company, having someone to encourage us, or even reading inspiring quotes that help us reflect on life's many blessings. For me, listening to Gospel music and videos keeps me uplifted. It's nice to be reminded that God's love is enough to be thankful for. God loves us. He walks with us. He hears our cry as well as our prayers. Having God makes everything so much different.

To wake up in the mornings knowing that your wake up is the first blessing of your day, that's being thankful. What's not to be thankful for? Strive to be thankful. I don't care what your today entails. Just know that everyday has a different lesson or blessing in it just for me and you. Looking back over the things that God has already brought you from is enough to be thankful. The Lord wants us to have a spirit of gratitude in all we do and say. When we are thankful and grateful, we will have greater happiness in our lives. The Prayers of protection, transformation and restoration will help you to discover a way of life empowered through the presence of God.

💡 Thought for Today:

Being thankful isn't just for the day. When you find yourself overwhelmed with worries of tomorrow, Praise God for who He is. He promises to never leave or forsaken us. Always keep that in mind.

♪ The Song of the Day: Thankful by: Mary Mary

Day 13

God's Word is Everlasting

Matthew 17:20 "Truly I tell you, if anyone says to this mountain, Go throw yourself into the sea; and doesn't doubt in their heart but believes that what they say will happen it will be done for them.

What does this scripture really mean to me? Jesus says that if you have faith, you can command a mountain to jump into the sea. Whatever you ask for in prayer, believe it and receive it and it will be yours in God's perfect timing. Sometimes I think that I say things just to say them when it doesn't happen for me. Other times, I question whether or not I put in the work of prayers. Did I not believe or not apply more faith to the situation? Was it not God's timing? Though I have questions in moments of despair, I am sure that God does things for our good. Whether it feels good or not. There's a plan in place and God has the ultimate plan. Other times, I say them and receive great results.

We have to be very careful what to ask of God, because if we ask for things with no faith then there's nothing to receive. I am always asking and a lot of times God makes it happen. Then, I wonder what I didn't receive was it because I didn't believe? You may too have the same questions. What I do now is put my faith in every situation and apply prayer on top of it no matter what it looks like or how it feels. If I believe it is going to happen for me, then it will. I'm sitting in a still moment waiting for these results of something I know God will give me. I also know that it is a process and things work according to God's plans and not mines. Some days, I say "Ok, God. Why is this situation taking so long when I got confirmation that it will be mine? I believed it. I prayed hard only to be turned away at the door. I was heartbroken and confused. I had everything I needed to have for that door to open for me. When You said it was for me."

Who said it was for you? Did God say it was for you or did you say it was for you? I had to realize during this experience that even if you get all the way to the door and it won't open, it simply means that the timing wasn't right. God was saving me from something that was behind that door. Numerous things went on in my mind. Even doubt kicked in a few times. I got all the way to the finish line and still didn't win. Abandonment tried to creep up but the Holy spirit wasn't having it.

"Keep the faith no matter what the outcome of a situation looks like, Nikki".

God wants us to be stable in our faith just like a tree deeply rooted into the ground or like this scripture speaks of a mountain. Mountains don't move. They are the ultimate symbol of stability. When Jesus speaks of mountains being moved or even dramatically thrown into the sea as a result of faithful prayers (Matthew 17:20; 21:21), He is deliberately invoking human impossibility. I'm just thankful enough for this experience because if I never went through it, I would never know that even when it doesn't work in my favor, I can still have faith in all things good.

💡 **Thought for today:**

Remember everything you will experience in life, you will overcome in life.

♫ **Song of The Day: Never be the same by Kelontae Gavin**

Day 14

The Still Moment

Exodus 14:14: "Just stay calm. The lord will fight for you; you need only to be still, the lord shall fight for you, and you shall hold your peace."

Good lord, it's so amazing how God is putting this book together with the stuff I wrote some time ago and it's speaking to my present self. Just stay calm. The Lord will fight for you. Do you know how many times I just repeated those very words time and time again? Do you know how many times I've said it today? It isn't easy staying calm when someone tries to play on your intelligence and they try to play on your growth. Stay calm because the Lord is going to fight for you and me.

Doing your best to walk right is NOT for the weak. Being still gives me time to think, to listen and to wait on His response. Being still means that I know that God is with me and leading me. Being still says that I am faithful and that I need, love and trust God. This scripture puts me back on the right path. I have been all over the place trying to do things my way and trying to get ahead of where God had wanted me. This scripture (Exodus 14:14) came after God felt that I had finished all of my running around. That's my take and I'm sticking to it. There were so many things that had been trying to keep me off track. It had gotten so bad that I started neglecting my home. I didn't see that every time I would go against the path chosen for me that I would turn up empty handed. It wasn't just throwing my positive progress off course. It was also delaying the process to be much farther than I was when I decided to take matters in my own hands.

Delay is the result of off the course wrecks. I know we have all gone off course a time or two. But God has other plans. I hear it loud and clear, "Be still and allow me [God] to fight for you. Let me lead you and you just follow me." The Holy Spirit was speaking. Once I repented, prayed and remained obedient to being still, I began to see favor in all of my situations. Everything that I spoke came to life. I'm still seeing this message "Be Still". That means I still need to remain quiet in this season of my life. God hasn't finished with me. There's more in the still moments to come. I hear You, Father. Nothing is moving in my eyesight, but I know God is working. I can hear Him so clearly now because there's nothing else that can distract me. God has stopped a lot of movement in my direction but I know He's up to something. If you take nothing else from this message of mine, take this. Don't get worked up, weary or angered by people. Don't you dare try to fight back. God promised us he'll do the fighting for us so let Him win for you.

☀ Thought for Today:

Be still so you can hear from the Lord. Just because you have a still moment from time to time and everyone around you is moving and prospering doesn't mean God isn't moving in your favor. There's favor, and restoration in your still moment. There are blessings and healing in your still moment. Whatever you do, don't rush where you are supposed to be in this season of your life.

♪ Song of the Day: Major by Jekalyn Carr

Day 15

Identify Yourself

Where are you at this very moment in your life? Have you changed for the better or have things taken a turn for the worst? If so, what are you going to do about it today? Right now, I'm in the transitioning stage. Not dying but transitioning into who God is birthing in me. I am being obedient enough to follow His path for my life. I'm looking and talking better while living out the best life I know how. There's so much I had to go through to get to this transitioning phase. I say what I been through a lot because it blesses me to speak about my past. I've overcome so many obstacles that others couldn't have. Throughout this book you may hear me going through things. You may read about me repeating some cycles in this book but one sure thing that you won't read about is me giving up. Still, I rise through Jesus Christ who strengthens me. I had to be still as I transitioned so I could see, feel and hear God moving in my life.

I am one to talk a lot but had to shut up so I could hear from God. If you are in this stage, here are a few things that helped me. First, you must take yourself outside of the equation and let the Holy Spirit go before you. A lot of times that's where we mess up. We allow the flesh to take full control of situations and life experiences instead of the Holy Spirit. The Holy Spirit exalts Christ in our hearts. He formed the image of Christ in us. We owe all to God in Salvation.

The father gave us the Son. The Son gave His life for us and the Spirit gives us life and faith in Christ. That why we must stay in the Word so we can know and grow. I'm learning new things right now as I'm typing up this Devotional. I wanted to pay someone to type my Devotional up because I didn't know how to type fast, and it was only going to slow my process in completing this book in a timely manner. I know it could be done quicker if someone else had done it, but God had other plans. Plans for me to learn to do some things on my own and to be able to stand on His word. The word says "I can do all things through Christ who strengthens me". Habakkuk 2:2-3 KJV, says "the Lord answers me and says to write the vision, make it plain upon tables that he may run that reads it." He wanted me to type this devotional myself so that I would see the picture God has for my life. Know the plan He has for you and then go after it full force, giving it everything you got. Just commit to God's call with your whole heart.

☀ Thought for Today:

Make your vision so clear that even if fear tries to come your way you wouldn't even recognize it.

♪ Song of the Day: Won't let Go by Travis Greene

Day 16

Temptation

Temptation is the desire to do something, especially something wrong or wise. Temptation defined in the bible is a situation in which one experiences or challenges to choose between fidelity and infidelity to one's obligations toward God.

God is never unfaithful to His own word. How do you overcome temptation from the Bible standpoint? Is it to turn to Him in Repentance? Do you meditate on God's word and avoid tempting situations?Are you being transparent to God and others? Temptation is a very deep topic for so many reasons. It is a part of everyday life. It is a choice. I keep revisiting the same temptation repeatedly. The only thing different in the things that tempt me is that they come in different ways. I'm not even sure why I have to be a Repeat offender to so many life situations such as this one right here, being tempted. God removed my most harmful temptation that I had ever experienced. It was gambling. I ate, slept and dreamt this thing. Some days were stronger than others but as soon as Satan saw me hot on God's trail here, he came in a different way. I knew right from wrong. My lifestyle changed drastically forcing me to become a borrower instead of a lender. It was very uncomfortable to say the least. Because I was one of God's favorites, I just knew whatever I did God would make it happen for me. Even if I did things that weren't pleasing to Him, I knew He would forgive me and bless me at the same time because I was this good person who did right by people. My thinking was misconstrued. This is what happens when you're desperate for a thing or trying to rush the process like I was. I was moving way too fast before God could even bless me, settling, playing Russian roulette with my finances.

Desperation breeds disaster. It will make you think about all sorts of things. I knew that I had to get a grip on myself. Remember, I was never a person who gambled with my life like I was doing. I prayed it wouldn't work immediately, because I still ran to my favorite spot thinking I was going to be Lady Luck only to leave the casino empty handed. I remember it like it was yesterday. I heard a voice say "don't go". Of course I ignored the voice saying "every time you come out there, you're going to leave with nothing".Everytime, that is what happened. I didn't even have enough money to pay the toll. As I walked to the car, I began to pray to God. I said to God, "if you take this addiction away from me, I promise to never pick it back up". From that day, I haven't had the desire to go back to that spot to gamble. Well, I will go on Sundays to pick up the free gifts they give to me for being a top tier member. Today, I don't even entertain those things anymore. I would never do myself like that again. Not even for a gift.

It was so easy to revisit temptation when you stop trusting God.Instead of taking my hard earned money and throwing it away on bad habits, I'm learning to solely depend on God now. God couldn't bless my gambling past. Those seeds weren't sown on fertile grounds. A harvest couldn't come from that. God gives us what we deserve. Temptation gives us temporary satisfaction. Allow God's will to be done in your life. That's when things will start happening for you. Be anxious for nothing but in everything by prayer and supplication, with thanksgiving, let your request be made known to God and the peace of God, which surpasses all understanding. Guard your hearts and mind through Christ Jesus (Philippians 4:6-7 NIV).

☀ Thoughts for Today:

You must know and stand on God's Word, and obey God's command in order to receive God's blessings.

♪ Song of the Day: You will win by Jekayln Carr

Day 17

The Overcomer

Take A Page Out of My Book is another journal that I write in. My personal and private thoughts and experiences are in that book. I jot down my daily happenings, whether good or not. This Devotional is me personally, but **Take A Page Out of My Book** is a little more detailed. Overcoming things that may be attached to you aren't the easiest. When you put your mind to it, All things are Possible through Jesus Christ who strengthens us. You won't always figure that out at the beginning of the process. I didn't figure that out until after the fact. After the stupid decisions or foolish ways. Those unappreciative relationships and Friendships taught me well. It can be extremely hard breaking away from people, places and things. Most things that you break away from are much needed. That is the part of overcoming. I was experiencing all types of obstacles trying to run away from the Old me. How was I going to encourage people when I was barely encouraging myself? One minute, I'm a "Godly" girl, the next minute I'm in the "World" again.

The cycles just kept repeating themselves over and over. IThat was all that 'free will' I was choosing to use instead of God's will for my life. Remember, God gives us the "free will" to do what's right. I have no clue because I was so hardheaded. Why did I mistreat myself? Why did I allow others to mistreat me? Today, Nikki, I speak life over you right now. All that you have overcome, let it be healing to your soul, and be fire to set someone else free. Be healed,Nikki,even if you must revisit a similar situation this time you can do it with wisdom, and knowledge of knowing your worth. You are greater than what you've been through. Just know it was God's grace & mercy that kept you from falling and giving up. I apologize to you for all that you had to endure. Going through was the hard part. Knowing better is the lesson learned.

No one has the right to ever misuse me again. I have the right to walk away from any harm, hurt or danger that comes my way. That's the "free will" that God gives me. Again, I apologize to anyone who has ever been hurt or is feeling defeated. Take your place of knowing who you are and whose you are. That's when you find your worth and unleash your peace. I love you and God does too. My healing is in this Devotional.

💡 Thought for Today:

Yes, it is true you can heal from the things you've been through. Sometimes, you can think you're healed from a place until you must revisit it again. What you overcame didn't define you as a person. You will succeed whatever is trying to hold you bound. Just know that you shall conquer and defeat what was in your way. If you did it once you can do it again. When you're Healed from some things, it won't affect you like it did before your healing took place. To God be the glory for all He's done for me.

🎵 Song of the day: You're the Lifter by Missionary Baptist cChurch

Day 18

Confirmation

Philippians 4:12-13 NIV: "I know what it is to be in need and I know what it is to have plenty. I have learned the secret of being content in any and every situation, whether well fed or hungry. Whether living in plenty or in want. I can do all this through Him who strengthens me."

I remember attending a 7:45 Zumba class at my church. The workout was so fulfilling. I guess I was just excited because I had never taken a Zumba class before. I was looking forward to the class and was so excited we got there before time. Everything was what I expected. I was able to keep up with all the excitement going on around us in the gym and with all the twists and turns. The music was great. The instructor was fun and full of life but it got even more interesting. I noticed that I was dancing on a scripture painted on the gym floor in bold red letters. Red is my favorite color. My heart told me it was going to be a word for me. Of course, I had to google it, because I'm fresh in my bible walk. I didn't have a clue what the Scripture was about to say to me. No one knew I was now gathering Bible scriptures to learn for myself and was excited about it. Looking down and seeing that scripture felt like God was there. I felt like He was speaking to me.

At the end of class, I googled Philippians 4:12. What it said spoke to my heart. If I never took anything serious, I knew from that day that God wasn't coming off the throne to tell me anything, but he would use signs to communicate with me. It was confirmation for my current experiences. I had to be content in all situations. It is important to rely on God's strength even where others are ready to help you during difficult times. When you fully trust in Him, He'll walk alongside you. God knows this message blessed my heart just by typing it. I pray it blesses the person who's reading it.

💡 Thought for Today:

There are many scriptures people choose to live by and never forget but one of the most well-known bible verses that often stands out or is well quoted is "I can do all things through Christ who strengthens me." You must know that it's not just Scripture or words but God's promise.

🎵 Song of the Day: Immediately by Tasha Cobbs

Day 19

Just Imagine

Try and form a mental image of some of the things I went through as I traveled this world called life. Just imagine stepping out on faith to start your own business and you decided to leave your job after 15 years to finally pursue your dreams. Close two years later, I packed all of my dreams up with no hard feelings. I didn't ask God "why" or "why did this happen" because that wasn't my purpose, I was just a visitor passing through that season of my life, I learned some very valuable lessons. I learned that I'm capable of running a business and being in touch with my creative side. God showed me there's more in store for me. Also imagine death coming into your family tree year after year for 4 years in a row with no breaks in between. The hardest death was losing the matriarch of the family, my Grandma Mable. I'm surviving off of the things she instilled in me.

Nikki, I'm never going to have to worry about you because you know how to survive. There's no way I could crumble as she left me with great comfort even after she's now gone. Then, there was one of my favorite Aunts. Aunt Margie was more like a sister to me. I can't even tell you the fun stuff she had me doing at a young age. Just know that she was that kind of Aunt. A year later I lost my dad aka My Baby Jesus. Our redefined relationship was like he was Jesus's cousin to me. Going to him for advice meant that I was going to get a word from the bible and he wasn't going to sugarcoat nothing for you. My Uncle passed a year later and then Aunt Edith, my first favorite aunt on my dad's side. Lord knows I miss her. She was a mother figure and my friend. Aunt was an understatement. By the time I got to her death, I began to understand that death was a part of life. Even though I wanted them all here, God had other plans.

It seemed as though nothing was working to help heal my pain from all those great losses. Some of you may be able to say you had similar situations or worse. For those of you who haven't, just imagine. Imagine some of my truth that didn't kill me but only made me stronger. Just imagine going through the same situations over and over with no lessons learned. Just a ball of confusion. Not knowing what to do or even how to do it, because your eyes have been closed for so long. When God finally opens your eyes so you can see those things Clearly that you once couldn't see, your situation changes. Your relations with others and outlook on things has changed. You now are having to choose the right path to walk and what company to keep. Just imagine losing someone that you thought was forever but wasn't ready for change. Imagine these life experiences that made your walk with God that much closer.

Just imagine if you didn't have to imagine and just relied on proverbs 3:5-6. Where would you be? If you can't imagine that, know that if God did it for me, imagine what He'll do for you. If you're going through anything that's too hard for you to bear, keep going and be patient through your process. God is going to see you through it. It's written here for you to see. If you need more clarity, Proverbs 3:5-6 (ESV) reads "Trust in the Lord with all your heart, and do not lean on your own understanding. In all your ways acknowledge him, and he will make straight your paths." This scripture means for us to trust God with all we have and not to depend on our own ways. Include God in everything that you do. This way you're giving Him a chance to keep you on the right path. We may not always know what's ahead of us but God knows what's best for us. If we just believe and rely on God when things don't go our way that increases our faith in Him. Trust that He's watching over us and guiding our daily paths as we do our best to move on.

Having faith in difficult times can allow you to find peace in God's presence. When we are unfaithful, it can harden our hearts with pride and cause us to grow farther from God. We must learn to give our problems and struggles to God so those things can be lifted off us. Imagine if we did everything God has said for us to do. We wouldn't have to imagine what the outcomes of our situations would be like because God would have His way with it.

☀ Thought for today:

What we think, we become. If all our thoughts came to life, just imagine what your world would look like. If you can think it, you can do it. If you believe in it, you can receive it. It's not just a motto. It's manifesting it into the universe.

♪ Song of the day: Imagine Me by Kirk Franklin

Day 20

The Way God Do Thangs

Romans 1:19-20 NLT: "They know the truth about God because He has made it obvious to them. For ever since the world was created, people have seen the earth and sky. Through everything God made, they can clearly see his invisible qualities- his eternal power and divine nature. so, they have no excuse for not knowing God.

What may be known about God is plain to them because God has made it plain to them. They exchange the truth of God for a lie and worship and serve created things rather than the creator who is forever praised. How is God made known? Through His mighty deeds and His interaction with his people. Throughout time, God has revealed Himself through creating the first human beings and their descendants. He reveals Himself through acts of history and interacts with us. God has shown Himself to me many times and I'm sure He's done the same for you. We want to run around and thank all the people we know and see doing things for us but be slow to thank God for all He's done. I'm speaking for myself as well.

God made all things possible. I was trying to figure out where in the world did everyone go in my life and I couldn't figure it out. I'm always there for everybody else and now I can't even buy some company. Were they running away from me because of my change? Was their time up? I didn't know what to think. After looking at things, I realize that this is God's way of showing me Him. Maybe He knew if I had others around me I wouldn't even notice His presence. Remember it is a choice to choose God. Now, I'm walking and talking with God daily. I'm praying and crying with God. Realizing today that He had to set me apart from others so I could see Him through his good works. Get to know Him for yourself so no one must tell you about Him.

☀ Thought for Today:

There will come a point in your life when things may seem a bit too much. When and if that time comes, trust in the Lord with all your might. Know there's nothing that is too hard for our God. If you would just believe in His word and stand strong on God's promise everything will turn out for your good and His glory.

♫ Song of the Day: Open Heaven by Maranda Curtis

Day 21

Let's Praise God

Let's praise God for life. Only the living can praise the Lord today. We are looking at God for increase and its impact on our lives. When something increases, in layman's terms, it simply means that it must move to another level. Psalms 115:12-15 says "The Lord Remembers us and will bless us. He will bless His people Israel. He will bless the house of Aaron. He will bless those who fear the Lord small and great alike. May the Lord cause you to flourish both you and your children. May you be blessed by the Lord, the maker of heaven and earth."

God promised us the blessed life, He wants to give us more wisdom, joy, peace, favor, love, and spiritual discernment, strength and faith. How are you going to receive these things? You must obtain the word of God by the studying of the scriptures and by your faith. That means before you see the answer or experience it, you receive the promise as true in your heart. You stay diligent in trusting God during the waiting period. We must believe in the promises that God has set before us. I pray every single morning and night a prayer of a blessed life for me and my kids. What mother wouldn't say that with the way of the world today?

The more you inhale God's word, the better your life will become. Your faith becomes stronger. Nothing we go through we'll go through alone. God provides help when we need it and even when we don't deserve it. That's the kind of God we serve. Your faith and trust are the pillars of dependence on God. We already depend on God for everything now. From waking us up in the mornings to covering us throughout the day, to the air that we breathe, to the food on our tables, and the jobs that supply our needs. Everything is done by God. Always give Him all the Praise.

🔆 Thought for Today:

In your weakest moments, your hardest battles, your saddest times and even those lonely nights, know you're NEVER alone.

🎵 Song of the Day: Something Good by Anthony Brown

Day 22

Ground Zero

Ground Zero. The lower level. The bottom. Whichever one you choose to call it. This is a place I had to go on my spiritual walk. There's nothing wrong with being in that place especially if you're looking at it in the spiritual realm of things. Ground Zero is a place where you will experience, grow and be stretched, disappointed, hurt and even confused at times. It's a learning place. Things will fall off at Ground zero. Old things will pass away at Ground Zero. New things will start happening for you at Ground Zero. Things will all start to make sense there.

It's a place where only me and God went. It served a purpose for my today, as well as my well-being. That was the only way I was going to see people, places and things through the spiritual realm. I was so used to looking at things with my flesh eyes or with blinders on. This is the fastest way to lose yourself or get off track. I lost my way looking at everything in the flesh. Ground Zero is a starting point for a new beginning. Ground Zero strips you of everything but you won't lose your Strength there you'll only become Stronger along the way. That's where you begin to see things differently, you'll start seeing God removing and replacing people, places and things in and out of your life before elevation begins. You'll need to release some things that won't be able to go with you to the next level.

You can't elevate with the weight of the world on your shoulders, distractions, or people that don't appreciate you or aren't meant for your destiny. You'll let go of those trying to hold on to you for their own financial gain or comfort. You can't elevate being stuck in the same place or mindset doing the same things. Elevation requires new levels, people and places to go. The Bible says in Joshua 3:7-8, "And the Lord said to Joshua, this day I will begin to exalt you in the sight of all Israel, that they may know that, as I was with Moses. so I will be with you". It was said that Joshua was faithful to Moses for 40 years and when it came time to pass the mantle to Joshua, God knew He needed to elevate Him in the eyes of the people in order for Joshua to accomplish his purpose. That is the purpose for elevation so that you and I can fulfill our purpose and our mission in life. Only God can elevate us spiritually, mentally, physically, and financially.

Who wouldn't want God to elevate them? Especially when He has the whole world in His hands. Trying to elevate ourselves before God, we can cut ourselves short of God's plan for our lives. Just think about where you are right now and how many people aren't with you at this present time. How many places you no longer go or some of the things you no longer do because you are where you are in this season of your life. You're rising up because you are leaning and depending on God. At Ground Zero, you can see things and remove things that wouldn't be as harmful as they would if you were at the top tier. Release at Ground Zero so when you get to the top you won't have to work as hard to remove things. Go up in life carrying only your weight. It will be less of a hassle.

💡 Thought for today:

Let God elevate you in His timing so you can be successful on time. God's timing is perfect timing.

🎵 Song of the Day: Look at Me Now by Pastor Mike Jr

Day 22

Testing, Testing

James 1:12 God's Word Translation (GW) "Blessed is those who endure when they are tested. When they pass the test, they will receive the crown of life that God has promised to those who love him. blessed is the man who remains steadfast under trial for when he has stood the test, he will receive the crown of life which God promised to those who loved him".

Blessed is a word culture has overused and misunderstood. This scripture that I stumbled across was speaking to my situation right now. This is why I am not moved by the situations surrounding me. Because of God's promise that even during the hardship, the hurt, the deceit, the backstabbing, the faking, the fronting, the lies and the self-inflicted wounds that we pile up on ourselves or just things that life throws our way, God wants us to trust Him. Trust him no matter what it looks like. No matter how it feels, He wants us to stand on His promises, but the thing is when you're going through why it is just that hard to do. If we just stand on His word, He shows up like He always does. Whether it's the death of a loved one, He's there. God will always comfort us with words of encouragement, with people and signs of confirmation. I'm still struggling with why it is so hard to stand when you're going through a test. You cannot have a testimony without one. That is something that I constantly tell myself when things that I'm going through are beyond my control.

God's grace and mercy will prevail always. After each test, I become a better student. It stretches my faith. It makes me rely on the promises of God. When we have hope, our rewards to come will be worth it. I know I can endure. You can also endure whatever trials and tests that come your way. Just remember that if you live, you will be faced with tests. Some are more extreme than others but through them all you will grow from them.

☀ Thought for Today:

Believe in your heart that every life experience that may come your way is just another obstacle you will overcome.

♪ Song of the day: New by Tye Tribbett

Day 23

The Good

Philippians 4:8 (NIV) "Finally, Brothers and Sisters, whatever is true, whatever is noble, whatever is right, whatever is pure, whatever is lovely, whatever is admirable – if anything is excellent or praiseworthy- think about such things."

What I took from Phillippians 4:8 is to think only good things as if it's so. Think about good things for your personal victory in every situation. It's so easy to dwell on the negative things that life throws your way. It's easy to focus on the hurt. That's why it's very important to know what the Bible says. Did you know everything that you will ever experience in life is written in the Good Book? The Bible instructs us on how to get through anything life may blow our way. The Bible is here to help us through the tough times and shows us even through those times that good will always outweigh the bad. If we never know the goodness of God, we sure need to know that the enemy comes to kill, steal and destroy. He knows all the tactics to use to knock us off course to the point. You won't even realize it's him doing it. You'll start to believe in those traps the enemy wants to set for you and then react ungodly, with anger and sadness or any other things that seek to separate you from the love of God. Even up to this day. I've been doing my best to practice the things of God. The more I seek God, the more the enemy tries his hands to test my faith in God. The enemy recognizes that

God is our greatest protection against the enemy's lies. When you feel you're being tested, you should remember the words of Jesus. Our father is greater than all. Romans 8 says "nothing, not death, life nor circumstances. Nothing can separate us from the love of God. Absolutely nothing."

☀ Thought for Today:

The Bible tells us everything we need to know about God and God's Love. Agape – unconditional "God's" love.

♫ Song of the day: Great Big God by Lisa Knowles-Smith

Day 24

Dropping a Jewel

Being Determined

You must make up your mind that whatever it is you want to accomplish you can do it. Being determined takes a strong mind. No matter how hard it is, be determined enough to get it done. Every time I thought about giving up, I heard the Holy Spirit say just as clear "I CAN DO ALL THINGS THROUGH CHRIST WHO STRENGTHENS ME". I knew if I had heard that inner voice that God had His hands on me to give me everything I needed to keep going, I knew I had enough strength to finish, to win and to get it done. Giving up should never be an option. If you fail at it, do it again. It's so easy to give in. I know there's so much more that God wants to give me. I can't receive it if I'm no longer wanting to Push through life to reap the rewards. In order to become successful, you must keep going. Life isn't going to give you anything freely. You have to earn it. Nothing feels better than a victorious win than to know you did all you could do to get to the top.

Keep going. Tell yourself again. Keep going. You got this. The only way to succeed in life is to always try again. My Goodness! I felt this jewel right here. I failed so many times in life and I promise to God not once did I ever want to GIVE UP. Yes, it was hard. Yes, I did hurt but giving up wasn't the answer. I remember running Track in High School. Though I lost a few races, it still made me better. I made a decision that I would just do better the next time. That's what I would tell my little self.

Growing up in life, I wanted to be so much. As a kid, I remember wanting to be Samantha on Bewitched way before I even knew what she was. I always wanted to make things happen but not realizing as a kid to an Adult now, that way was too easy. And nothing easy ever lasts. I had all types of gigs, dreams and aspirations growing up. From ND Vines Cleaning Service, where we clean newly built homes getting them ready for their new owners. Blocks of Blessings Day Care service to ND Vines Transportation, Panties and Bra Sisterhood Club, Little Diva Sorority to At the Spot Paint Studio and Divas Camp. None of it lasted. What it did do was build me up for the Women's Gathering movement to encourage, inspire and give hope to other women through my own personal experiences in life. I had to go through all those things to get to where I am today. It's like crawling before you walk. You must grow through your experiences and failures. If I had to do it all over again, I would. Failures are filled with lessons. You learn to be bigger and better than your last experience. Be Determined.

♪ **Song of the Day: God Did it Again by Branden Anderson**

Day 25

My Strength

Isaiah 58:11(NIV) "The Lord will guide you always; He will satisfy your needs in a sun scorched land and will strengthen your frame. You will be like a well-watered garden, like a spring whose water never fails."

This verse is filled with all promises of hope. The Lord will: You'll be guided continuously, satisfy your soul in drought, strengthen your bones, make you a flourishing garden and make you a never-failing spring of water. God is the source of all the strength you need at every stage in every season of your life. He is the restorer of your strength when your strength runs low. We have a source of strength that will undergird and sustain us in every way. Receive his strength today!

I want to be honest. I am standing in faith and prayer at this very moment of my life. I keep seeing miracles, signs and wonders and when I tell you God has truly given me signs, But before I move, I ask God to guide me. Even though He gives us free will to make wise choices, I want to make sure I'm doing as I'm supposed to for the next assignment. Surely, He comes through and connects the dots. The scripture says He'll turn your deadest situations into miracles and those times of desperations into peace. I know, no matter where I am in life or who I'm around, God is going to show up for me. I would normally fall apart from things that happened in my past but now when situations arise, I just smile, pray, keep believing and thanking Him for His grace and mercy on my life. There's nothing too hard for God especially once you get out of the way. That's when He can do his work through you and for you. Amen.

I'm truly thankful for this journey of learning who and where God is and how He speaks to me. I never knew it would be like this but I am grateful that God chose me to walk this path. Repeat after me: Father God in heaven, Thank you for showing up for me. Thank you for strengthening me. Thank you for holding on to me even when I don't make wise decisions. Through all of my situations, I want to say thank you. Thank you for Your guidance, love, peace and everlasting covenant over my life. I pray that I will continue to walk as You will have me to walk. Even if I go astray, I pray that you will forever keep your hands upon me in Jesuss name, I pray, Amen.

💡 Thought for today:

Know in life you can't take things so personal. Everything happens for a reason.

🎵 Song of the day: Repay Me by PJ Morton

Day 26

The Abandonment

Abandonment is the action or fact of being abandoned. It is the fear of losing connection with people you love which then forces you to fend for yourself. This is a deep topic for me. I pretty much kept this one personally between me and God. This topic is so needed to be talked about in today's world, and in households with parents working day in and out not realizing the effect it may have on their children. I know for me if you don't heal from these issues, they will only pour into other relationships that you may encounter or even become a trigger point. This happens to people with a history of trauma. I know it started as a child with Daddy issues and stuck with me well into adulthood. Once my dad got his life together, he apologized for not being the father that I needed to love and protect me the way I should've been loved and protected. Even though I was 32 years old when it happened, I felt the burden of the world lifted off my shoulders. I was now free. Our relationship went through the roof like nothing had ever happened between us. I thought because I had the best grandparents in the world that I didn't need my momma and daddy as much but I realized no matter how good my grandparents were on both sides of my Family, I still needed the love and affection from my own parents.

I began loving my grandma Mable as if she had birthed me and she knew that. I remember one time she told me that

I wouldn't love my own mom the way I love her until she passed away. That was deep but true. That lady never saw me any other way but as her child. Even in all my wrongdoing, there was never any love lost in her eyes, she would never say I was a handful or even threatened to send me back home to my mom. I needed all her love and attention. It was specially made. Not taking anything from my momma but it was a different kind of love coming from my grandma. As I got older, it got worse in a good way. I depended on her for everything. I needed her advice which was wisdom that I still use today. Her shoulder to lean on when times got a little hard. She was that person that would never judge and reassured me everything would be ok. I would ask her before I asked anyone else for things I wanted or needed. She was my comfort and I depended on her even as an adult.

It was Mother's Day 2014. I had just overcome abandonment issues a few years back and I was about to relive those issues again. A few hours after I left her, I received a phone call that she had passed away. Knowing that I was no longer going to see her pierced my heart. No one was going to love me like her. Who was I going to go to now to comfort me through life experiences? All types of things were going through my head. Sadness, anger and confusion to say the least. She had prepared me for this day already, but I wasn't going to understand that till after her death. She prepared me to have a relationship with God. She taught me how to stand on His word. But going through the death of a loved one can trigger abandonment issues.

You have to get in that word to be able to stand on it. The Scripture to stand on in this situation is **Deuteronomy 31:6 "Be strong and courageous. Do not be afraid or**

terrified, because of them, for the Lord your God goes with you. He will never leave you nor forsake you." Even after having a relationship with God, you may still revisit a triggering situation. This time it won't have you bound like it did when God wasn't a presence in your life. I'm telling you firsthand it just happened to me in my new walk with God on 7/22. I had a disagreement with my husband and we both went two separate ways with our decisions causing me to shut down on our relationship. It's when God takes the blinders off you, and you begin to see things as they are. After overlooking things for so many years to keep the trigger points from resurfacing because you know what kind of harm it could do to you if that abandonment issues rose. How far back it could set me mentally wasn't something that I wanted to relive. As much as I didn't want it to, it still happened. I got to be honest with you. I was filled with such disappointment with no return. My flesh and Spirit man went to war with each other but ultimately the Holy Spirit won. That's when I knew God had me. I wasn't just saying I was leaning and depending on God because I mentally and physically was. I felt alone in this at first because the flesh wanted some action, but the Holy spirit wanted me to stand on the word of God. So, when that trauma tried to creep in like a thief in the night,tThe Spirit said just as clear "Don't be terrified because of that past trauma and abandonment issues, but know that the Lord will never leave you nor forsake you."

Tell me God ain't good! Just like that, the Holy Spirit was activated and God fought that battle. My spirit is so full just writing about this trauma. Satan, you can't have a place where my Lord and Savior dwells. Heavenly Father, thanks for rescuing me in my time of need and in my time of despair. Thank you Lord for keeping Your hands on me. Keep me covered in your perfect will, Lord. To guide me and comfort me, Lord. Whatever you do, please don't take Your hands off me. Let Your will be done and all that You will continue to do in my life. I thank you Lord for the favor. Whatever you do, Lord, go before me that I may be reminded every day that I will never walk alone as long as I serve You. In Jesus' name, I pray for no more drama. No more trauma. In Jesus's Holy Name, I pray. Amen

💡 Thought for Today:

What are you going to do when things of the world start coming for you? You're going to stand on God's word. You're going to pray until things change.

🎵 Song of the Day: Pray by CeCe Winans

Day 27

A Mouth Full

Proverbs 18:21 (NIV) The Tongue has the power of life and death, and those who love it will eat its fruit.

The fruit of the spirit is love, joy, peace, faithfulness, kindness and self-control and patience. According to Proverbs, one should be very careful with his or her words and be slow to speak about the things that come out of it. I fully understand the power of the tongue and the words we should use to say good things so they can manifest from what we speak. I've spoken many things in existence starting at a young age. A lot of what I thought and spoke came to life. From my childhood boyfriend who became my husband. If you believe it, speak it and it can be. I watched my business @the Spot being birthed with every word I spoke over it. I've also messed up a lot of things by speaking poorly and not having the wisdom at the time to know better. Even knowing that scripture and the things I was taught about like the saying "if you don't have nothing nice to say, don't say nothing at all". How easy is it if you don't have Proverbs 18:21 to go by?

The saying "sticks and stones may break my bones, but words would never hurt me". is not a fact. If I knew what I know now then the things people said or thought of me wouldn't have mattered. I've had my feelings hurt and have been heartbroken by people and family members who have said many hurtful, degrading things to me. It took me 47 years to realize people's words were just their words. Their words didn't validate me or who God created me to be. Those were years of not knowing and being immature to God's word. Also there was a time or two that I wasn't speaking from love, peace or kindness with my words. I became judgmental. When you know better, you'll do better. Getting to know God's word is making me better today because I have a choice to speak life into myself as well as into others knowing that what comes out of my mouth comes from my heart speaking. Good words say that my heart is clean. Speaking poorly or negatively is simply saying I have an Unclean heart and that's not of God. Remember God gives us "free will". Choose your words wisely and not out of a place of wickedness.

My thoughts for today:

Let your words be the peace someone needs today.

♫ Song of the Day: Forever is a long time. by Jason Nelson

Day 28

Pain and suffering in its PURPOSE

> Romans 8:28 And we know that God causes all things to work together for good to those who love God, to those who are called according to his purpose.

The promise of Romans 8:28 is that God works for our good "in all things" is reassuring. So, through the pain, hurt and discomforts of life and situations, there's purpose in why it happened and why pain was inflicted.

Pain is a localized or generalized unpleasant sensation, complex or emotional experience that may cause mild to major physical discomfort as well as emotional distress to the mind and the body. It is that mental and emotional distress you feel from a loss of a loved one, or even those closest to you that mistreated you, deceived you and hurt your heart to the core. I won't say that I'm a pro at the pain and suffering department, but I'm very familiar with feeling the pain in the mind, body and heart. Sometimes, I became numb to it because it was the same situation. The pain was the same each time. But once you experience enough pain repeatedly, you become accustomed to it. Pain will have your mind all over the place, having you want to give up on things, walking around like an air head with no thoughts inside the brain. I'm just telling you about me so remember while you're reading this devotional these things are about me, what I've been through and how I got set free.

God knows pain isn't the easiest to heal from so go through with the word of God. Everybody's arrival time to heal is different. Your pain is your pain and no one can tell you how to feel in your pain or how to love in your pain but the word of God can. Know that your pain and suffering can come to you so that God can get the Glory. I know you don't understand but hold up let me finish. I'm telling you what I witness from the self-inflicted pain I've embedded in myself and the pain I allowed others to inflict on me as well. It's crazy how once you become a new creature and rely on God's word then things will become different. You'll accept different things and walk and talk differently. It's not one thing that I would change about my life, NOT one thing I've been through. Going through makes you appreciate your past. It gives you a step to stand on to get you to the next level in life. I'm filled with excitement and joy because I've been through hell and back and God never took His hands off me. There's purpose in my pain. That's with everything I've been through., People need to know how I'm able to forgive. Purpose captures the heart of why we are on this earth and why Jesus died for us. Purpose defines your life and not on your terms but God's terms. How are you going to walk in your purpose if you have never experienced pain?

☀ Thought for today:

Understand that it takes time to heal from pain. There's no fast way to heal from it. Deal with what hurt you in the first place. Allow your emotions to flow. Talk about it. Pray about it but don't stay in your hurt long. It's written in the bible that weeping may endure for a night, but joy comes in the morning. (Psalms 30:5)

♪ Song of the day: Shine, Shine, Shine by Zauntee

Day 29

Get out of God's Way

Psalms 86:1-7 A prayer of David (NLT) "Bend down, o Lord hear my prayer; Answer me, for I need your help. Protect me, for I am devoted to you. save me, for I serve you and trust you. you are my God. Be merciful to me, o Lord, For I am calling on you constantly. Give me happiness, O Lord for I give myself to you. O Lord, you are so good, so ready to forgive, so full of unfailing love for all who ask for your help. Listen closely to my prayer, o Lord; Hear my urgent cry. I will call to you whenever I'm in trouble and you will answer me."

When I read this scripture, it said my entire name, my situations and more. I love the way the Bible speaks to every one of my needs. There's nothing that has happened in your life that hasn't already happened in life, or the bible. You can find yourself or your situations and how to resolve it in the Bible. God is the Author of it. The Bible can be your healing place. I had no clue what was going on in my life and as I'm starting to piece things together, I'm realizing so much about God. I was in a situation where I needed a whole lot of help and all I could do was worry and be filled with frustration. I did know which way to turn, but didn't do it at the beginning of my situation. It wasn't until the situation became too unbearable and I had enough of myself, I said "Lord, help me please.", with so much urgency. "I don't know what's going on around me and today, I give it to You.

I believe in my heart that by putting it in Your hands, that You will make a way from me, Lord. That You will answer my prayers and that you will wipe away my tears."

    I was so busy getting in the way and trying to go before God. That is why I couldn't see what God was doing. This was only prolonging my situation to get fixed. God must go first, and you must follow Him so that you can see the work of the Lord. How does the song go," Can't nobody do it like Jesus". The Bible is your Source. Open it up and read all about it. Your situation and life can change in the blink of an eye. But God won't change. His promise won't change. Trust in the Lord with All your heart. Just know He's only a prayer away.

☀ The thought for today:

Get out your own way so God can use you. You make things harder than they should be when you're not obedient to the will of God. You won't know if you're disobedient if you don't know God. Get to know Him for your own good.

♬ Song of the Day: We Gon Be Alright by Tye Tribbett

Day 29

"Trust Him"

The moment you let go is the moment you'll begin to see the signs of God's presence in your life. It wasn't until I really let go and allowed God to take my hand in this new walk that I'm trying my best to perfect. I kept straddling the fence. One minute, I'm trusting God and the next minute, I want to be in total control while walking in the flesh. I was getting weary one minute then applying the faith the next. I finally made up my mind that if I wanted something different, I had to do something different. This required me fully trusting God. It always works better that way when He's in control. When it's done in that order, you tend to worry less. Situations you thought you had no control of, turn out in your favor. You can't take every situation in your own hands. I say it all the time. God has the whole world in His hands. Why get weary, Nikki? That's how I would talk to myself trying to convince the flesh to stand down to the spirit man. We all know how that pans out sometimes. The more you feed the spirit man the more the flesh must die. Matthew 15:28 (NIV) says "Then Jesus said to her, Woman, you have great faith! Your request is granted. And her daughter was healed at that moment." This was the perfect scripture to stand on as I was relying solely on God with none of my flesh interruptions. He doesn't come through for us because we deserve it. God comes through for us because that's who He is. He's so faithful to us even when we don't deserve it. Trust Him.

💡 Thought for Today:

Don't limit your knowledge of knowing who God is. You must know Him in order to trust in him. You will bear fruit that way. He'll be with you always and he'll always have protection.

♪ Song of the Day: You get the Glory By JJ Hairston & Youthful praise

Day 30

God first

Psalms 16: 8 (KJV) "I have set the Lord always before me: because he is at my right hand, I shall not be moved."

Once you learn the word of God, you'll understand putting God before yourself. Putting God first is in our hearts, in our prayers and something you should utilize daily. The more you put God first the more He becomes visible to you and all your needs. In 2014, I decided that I was going to walk, talk and breathe and sleep God. But if you have read this devotional, you know that a few times I failed. I failed at being a good steward. I failed by thinking I was perfect. Only God is perfect. Did it make me a bad person?No. It reminded me that I am human. As you become wiser in God's word, it teaches you about all your shortcomings and imperfections. Everything didn't change overnight but gradually it started happening.

    I was in church every day the church doors opened. Sundays and Wednesdays, you name it. I was there for women's Bible study groups at church. I just wanted something different. I wanted a change in my life. I got tired of the same old ways of mine. It wasn't taking me anywhere but down the same road. I started changing up the music I was listening to. I went from 92.1 to listening to 104.7. That was my new morning inspiration. I wanted to feed my soul well with no interruptions of worldly things because that's a quick way to get thrown off course. I was now filled with the hope and the promises of God. This was becoming justice for my new journey. Attending things only affiliated with God would help me to make less hiccups to the world's playground. The more of the word of God you inhale, the more you'll hear from the Holy Spirit. It's just as clear but you have to listen. You need to be attentive. God aligns things in our lives so perfectly through His word. Knowledge is Power. Get to know the Word of God for yourself so you can have the Power to overcome anything life brings your way. The word is going to keep you.

☀ Thought for Today:

Things aren't always the way they appear to be. God does things to blow your mind and so you'll know that it was Him that did it. Things can seem bad to you but God will turn things around just for your good. Don't beat yourself up about going through stuff. It's all for good reasons. Might be bad now, but God.

♪ Song of the Day: Pick Yourself Up by Amanda Black

Day 31

Intentional

Genesis 50:20 (NIV) "You intended to harm me, but God intended it for good to accomplish what is now being done, the saving of many lives."

When I read this scripture, I immediately start to think about all the times the enemy sat right in my company to get everything it could get out of me, just to use it against me. The enemy knows your weaknesses. If not he'll study you until he figures you out. The devil isn't dressed in a red outfit with spike ears and a long wide tongue. He has on a disguise standing right underneath your nose or right beside you. He can be just a phone call away or nearby. At least that has been my experience. The enemy has used the closest people who meant the world to me to get my attention. The Devil is clever and he comes to steal, kill and destroy. If that means using your kids, just know that he'll use them too. You won't even see it coming.

    I had this one family member that I truly cherished. Anything that she wanted or needed, I would have given it to her. While I loved her like a sister, I found out that she secretly hated me. She would go to any measure to try and defame my character. She was a liar. This girl was a repeat offender. If she thought that you knew or loved me, she would sow negativity about me. I couldn't figure out why. What did I do to someone so bad to deserve this type of treatment? My grandma kept trying to warn me about her. She said that the more I loved her, the more she was going to stab me in the back. Though she didn't physically stab me in the back, it sure felt as if she did with the way she spoke of me. Everybody was aware of it besides me. My eyes were blinded by her antics until after my grandma passed away. That's when her true colors showed up and those blinders came off my eyes (wisdom). Finally, I could see her for who she really was.

    When a person is filled with a lot of hurt and anger that's all that they can offer you. What's been afflicted on them will fall on you. You must remember that the devil doesn't love. I was full of love because that's who God is. Even if you hurt me, I would still love and forgive the same. Remember, the devil can quote Bible scriptures. The lesson to be learned was called standing on the word of God. (Genesis 50:20) "What was meant for your harm, God will use it to your advantage. If God is for you, who dare be against you. Always love your enemies. Do good to those who hate you. Bless those who curse you. Pray for those who mistreat you."

    Let us pray: Father God in heaven, thank You for never leaving me or taking Your hands off me even in my trying times. Thank You for always being my protection and my eyes when I could not see the danger around me. Thank you for every good and bad situation that I ever had to encounter because without them I wouldn't know You like I do. Father, thank You for Your mercy and grace on me. If I had to do life without it, I wouldn't be able to appreciate where I am today. Thank you for Your love, Father and thank You for the person who is reading this. I pray that this message gives someone hope today. If there's anything you're dealing with, put it in God's hands. Amen.

♫ Song of the Day: Made A Way by Travis Greene

Day 32

You are the Light

Matthew 5:14(ESV)"You are the light of the world. A city set on a hill cannot be hidden.

In this scripture, God is showing us the importance of letting the Gospel light shine in our lives. Light is defined as life as seen in John 1:4. "In Him was life and life was the light of men. Those who have faith through Him will have eternal life." This life is a gift from Jesus brought from God into a dying world. This Bible verse mirrors my life right now. Being in a dark place is what brought me closer to God. The more I included God, the more God's light started to shine in me. My prayer life started to change. I was no longer uneasy about praying because I knew God was going to give me every word, I needed to deliver my prayers into the universe.

My visits to church were more than just Sunday Morning Worship. Wednesday Bible Study was now teaching me more about God's laws and Commandments. I started doing the Morning Welcome. Now I am working with the Youth Ministry. I realize God placed me in this ministry because I was a beginner. This was the fresh start that I needed. The more I worked with the youth the more God started using me to speak and pray with and for my family and friends about the goodness of him (God). I believe the more I'm available the more God will use me. I pray that my light will continue to shine and draw others closer to Him through my walk and faithfulness.

Cut your light on so it can shine and others can see God working through you. If you are wondering how to do that, confess with your mouth that "Jesus is Lord". Believe it in your heart that God raised him from the dead and you will be saved. If you don't believe me, just read Romans 10:9(NKJV)

💡 Thought for Today:

Grateful is when you can just sit alone in your thoughts and think about how blessed you are. Nothing could be going on but you're just grateful. The fact that you're still here on Earth to enjoy all of God's creations is enough to be thankful for. You're blessed. Your family is blessed and full of life. That's being grateful.

🎵 Song of the day: Everlasting God by: William Murphy

Day 33

The Crown

Isaiah 40:29 (NIV) "He gives strength to the weary and increases the power of the weak. But those who trust in the Lord will find new strength. They will soar high on wings like eagles. They will run and not grow weary. They will walk and not faint."

This scripture speaks volumes to anything you have going on in your life. If it's death in your family, this scripture is one to stand on. If you're hurting or sick with health issues or things beyond your control, this scripture will get you through. It will get you through heartaches, confusion, doubt or fear. God will give you strength to endure, overcome and to see that He was the one that carried you through. That's the kind of God we serve. God gives a fresh supply of spiritual, supernatural strength and faith to those who have humble dependence on Him. When we try to get through trying times and difficulties while relying on our own strengths, we fail, become weary and unable to bear the burdens.

This message takes me back to the night my daughter's cousin was killed on her birthday. It was April 3, 2022. That night we celebrated a life of 30 years with family and friends. The atmosphere was so thick with love. Even the onlookers were engulfed in our love. That's the only way I can describe it. Pure love and positive energy. Those kids were all thirty and living their best lives. Lil Lakeith had turned thirty on January 21, 2022. He came out to celebrate with Kanesha for her 30th birthday. They were always there for each other. Watching them all grow up into respectful, well-mannered adults was truly a blessing. In the blink of an eye, they were crying at the loss of a loved one. How could this day filled with so much love turn into hate? As I reflect on that day, I realized that it was so perfect. The timeline couldn't have been any better. The memories of that day will last forever. Even though it was the ending of our loved one's life, it was perfectly made just for him. He went home to be with the Lord after loving on everyone. He would've been surrounded even if he knew it was his time to go.

Lil Lakeith did everything with a bang. Before he even made it to the brunch, he took his girlfriend on a little walk. During the walk, she placed a white flower in his left pocket as a love token. As he heads to the party, Lil Lakeith goes live to show Kanesha he's on his way to her. The video caption said "KNR I'm almost there". The sunroof was open. The wind was blowing through the car. The sun beaming down on him from the sunroof was so perfect. I promise I can't make this up. This is the beautiful stuff that God will do. As the video is playing, it captures the flower in his pocket fluttering from the outside wind blowing inside the car. Then the video goes off. A little while later, I saw his car fly by the restaurant window. Five minutes later, Lil Lakeith was coming through the front door like a breath of fresh air. Everyone was greeting and loving on him not knowing what was about to take place later. We embraced each other and as we were about to let go, I grabbed hold of him again. We told each other our "I love you ". As the party was ending, the cousins, Lakeith, and Lapooh helped carry Kanesha's birthday flowers and gifts to her car. At that moment, it appeared like some guys were following this beautiful woman with flowers down the street. I immediately asked them to stop to take a picture. It was so perfect.

A few hours had passed by and I found myself confused with mixed feelings and emotions. I received a phone call that I would've never expected. For two weeks, I was all over the place. My regular routine had been thrown off because of that night. It changed everyone connected to Lil Lakeith. As the scriptures come to life in my mind, heart and spirit, it gives some comfort. Isaiah 40:29 says "God is going to give you strength." To Lakeith's parents: read and believe the word. God's word is true. If He said he'll do it, know that He will. Weeping may endure for a night Lakeith &Tracey, but joy comes in the morning. I dedicate this scripture to you both. I know this won't be easy as your days turn into weeks and weeks turn into months. I pray that the Lord carries you through this valley of death with peace in your heart and the strength of the Lord. I can't imagine what pain you are feeling but what I do know is God's grace and mercy endures forever. I love you both and thank God for you.

💡 Thought for Today:

There's a process in everything new. Don't rush or force it. The timing of development is perfect.

🎵 Song of the Day: Another Blessing by Prince Tai

Day 34

Tempted

In this devotional, I wrote about temptation in the front of the book. As I'm coming to the end, temptation has come up again. It just showed up in a different way. Sometimes, in life you will revisit some situations because there is something else that you need to learn. Maybe it is testing your growth and seeing how you'll handle the situations once you have identified that it was" temptation". Writing this devotional has so many perks. I'm learning so much about myself. As this book is coming to a close, I am thankful for the growth. All of my experiences have brought me here. I know what I went through could be a blessing to someone else. I hope at least one page in this book has been useful.

> *1 Corinthians 10: 13: "The only temptation that you have are the temptations that all people have. You can trust God. He will not let you be tempted more than you can stand. But when you are tempted, God will also give you a way to escape temptation. Then, you will be able to stand it."*

Temptation is the devil trying to get us to do something wrong. God has promised to help us when we are tempted so that we can choose to do the right thing. It's when you seek God that temptation tries to rise in your life. I was minding my own business, studying the word of God, being more involved in church activities. I was praising God and having my own Bible studies. It was just me and God. I had learned to embrace this new relationship with my Heavenly Father. Hearing from the Holy Spirit was everything. It was fresh. I felt renewed.

Walking into something new can be so exciting and that's what I was doing. Trusting the process and allowing Him to lead the way. I often ask myself why I didn't build a relationship with God sooner. Then I remember that I arrived when I was supposed to and that's all that matters. Of course the enemy didn't care about any of that. He was determined to throw me of course. He knew what to do and who to use to get my attention: My Family. I became unguarded for the moment, and he drove in like a thief in the night. I allowed my flesh to take the lead. That's how he was able to get in my head.

Though he was there, I was still aware of his evil devices. My pastor had just preached about temptation right before things started to spiral out of control. Pastor Fred said that if you weren't grounded in the word of God, the devil would try his hands. All he needed was your mind. Good God Almighty! I was being prepared before it even happened. You can't tell me that wasn't God. I had to turn up the heat on Satan. I started praying even harder and reading the word a little more. I did all of the things that he despised. For years, he knew how to trick me. No more!

Devil in hell, I want you to know that you can not win in my life anymore. God has the whole world in His hands. That means that you can take every situation out of your hands and put it in God's hands and realize it's no longer your battle. We can go to a fight with the chance that we may or may not win. If God fights for you, he will win. Amen.

Let's pray: Father God in Heaven, thank You for being everything I need when I need it. I welcome You into my life and every situation in my life. Keep me covered in Your perfect will, Lord. Have Your way with me. Lord, guide me in the way that I should go from day to day. Whatever you do, please don't take Your hands off me, Lord. You're a miracle worker and a promise keeper. Keep me close to you, Father. Take control of the things I have no control over and have your way in them. I speak deliverance, favor, love, and peace over me, Lord. I pray good health, wealth and prosperity over me and those attached to me. In Jesus' Holy Name, Amen.

💡 Thought for today:

Don't worry about anything. God prepares us all for the things we will face in life. Rest assured He'll go before you and create a safe place for your arrival. All you must do is call out to Him for help. He'll guide you and take you right where you're supposed to be.

🎵 Song of the Day: Lord, You are Good by Todd Galberth

Day 35

"Faith"

Faith is belief and trust. People who have great faith in God do what He says to do, even when they don't understand why. They do it because they believe and trust Him. Faith in Jesus means believing He is the son of God and trusting in Him. You must have faith in the Lord. It is one way to stand strong. Standing strong when things become too much to bear, during the loss of a loved one, or just life experiences. Let your faith be bigger than your problems. If your faith is not strong, then you will not have strength to endure any of life experiences. You must trust God.

You have to have big faith but there are times where it is hard to trust the process or stand strong on God's word. Yet, it's truly the way. On Sunday, May 8, 2022 at our 8 a.m. church service, my Pastor and First Lady gave a sermon on exactly what I had spoken about a few days before. She spoke about every situation I had going on. She discussed how I was dealing with it and what it would do to me if I didn't do something about it. She was hot on my trail with each situation I had going on. I wanted to run around that church so fast, but I just stood there and inhaled the sermon, because I knew there were more instructions to come. It was truly a confirmation for me. God was acknowledging his presence through her. This sermon even spoke on the outcome. Every word she had spoken my outcome was just like it. Can't nobody tell me who Jesus is. Nobody, not even my troubles can make me doubt Him. Having the faith of knowing He'll turn my whole life around and watching what He's doing in my life now is enough to believe. Just believe and he'll do the same for you.

💡 Thought for Today:

Don't ask the question "why". You experience things to discuss with others. Share your faith.

♫ Song of the Day: For My Good by Judah Band

Day 36

Wherever You Are, God is.

I was reading the Bible this morning and what I read was the beginning of elevation and transformation for me. As I began to read this chapter in the Children's International Bible IBC version, it read, "Joseph goes to prison for being faithful to his king". Joseph remained loyal and steadfast. Faithfulness comes from a place of trust and loyalty. **Hebrew 11: 1** says "now faith is a confidence in what you hope for and assurance about what we do not see. As a Christian, it is important to be faithful to God. It is one thing to simply believe in Him but another to be faithful to Him. Joseph goes to prison because he chose not to sleep with his King's wife. What I learned from reading this scripture is that no matter where you are in life, God is going to be there. That could be a crack house or a gambling house. It doesn't even matter. That's the difference between God and man. God will forgive you and man will hold it against you even after you overcome it.

When you get discouraged in life or things don't go your way, just know God is with you everywhere you go. Through the pain, He's there. Through the heartaches He's there. When you don't understand, He's still right there. You can't see Him but He's right there when you need Him.

☼ **Thought for Today:**

Wherever you are God is. WHEREVER

♫ **Song of the Day: Now I Know by Ted & Sheri**

Day 37

The FIGHT

Exodus 17:8-16: "*Rephidim the Amalekites came and fought the Israelites. So Moses said to Joshua, "Choose some men and go and fight the Amalekites. Tomorrow, I will stand on the top of the hill. I will hold the stick God gave me to carry." Joshua obeyed Moses and went to fight the Amalekites. At the same time Moses, Aaron and Hur went to the top of the hill. As long as Moses held his hands up, the Israelites would win the fight. But when Moses put his hands down, the Amalekites would win. Moses arms became tired. So, the men put a large rock under Moses, and he sat on it. Aaron was on one side. Moses and Hur were on the other side. They held his hands up like this until the sun went down. So, Joshua defeated the Amalekites in this battle. Then the Lord said to Moses, "Write about this battle in a book so people will remember. And be sure to tell Joshua tell him because I will completely destroy the Amalekites from the earth". Then Moses built an Altar. He named it The Lord is My Banner. Moses said, "I lifted my hands towards the Lord's throne. The Lord will fight against the Amalekites forever."*

I could really relate to this story. I saw so much of myself in this chapter. What stood out the most was Moses being obedient to God and he had two friends, partners and brothers on earth to help him in a time of need. My heart filled with so much joy because I was in a fight and I thought I was about to lose it all. My pride had gotten in the way and

I didn't want to share it with others. I kept it to myself until it became too much to bear. That's when I finally released it to my close family and friends and they all came to my aid like no other. I had cried out to God so much about the situation and thought because I put myself in that predicament, it was over for me. But, God showed up for me. My family and friends showed up to the point that it was an overflow. There was nothing but favor from God.

I can't do anything but praise His Holy name. He's shown up for me even in fights I brought upon myself. God knows he did. My family and friends came and picked me up because I had fallen. Yes, me. The one who's there for everybody and through everything. I had fallen and they came to rescue me. I'm not talking about a little fall. I fell where I needed several people to pick me up and it was so perfect that everybody was available at the same time to assist me. Just like Moses' friends did. it was nothing but the man upstairs looking down on me. It was this situation that helped me walk with God even more. God will show Himself to you. Go through something and see where your help is going to come from. That's why it is important to get in the word of God. It will guide you in your time of need, trouble and confusion. You don't have to search very far. He's available at all times. If you ever get into a fight or trouble, call on Him to fight your battles. It's already won.

💡 Thought for Today:

You don't have to get ready for a fight. Get on your knees and say a prayer.

🎵 Song of the Day: I Made It by Da 'TRUTH

Day 38

The Fight Continues (Repeat Offender)

Soon as you're over one hurdle here comes another one. The thing is to learn from what you've been through, or you'll become a repeat offender. I've been in this fight here for a long time on repeat. I've learned something from the first fight that I wasn't doing in this fight. Again, this is why I'm stuck on repeat. That prayer life that you built, the wisdom that you gain, yes that's what you'll need in this fight Nikki, yes. I'm talking to myself. This is how I get through. Just me and the Holy spirit. See, I didn't have the Holy Spirit the last few fights but I got Him now. At this point in my life, I'm seeking the Lord to get me through all obstacles. I don't want to waste another minute on fighting or dealing with dead situations. This has been my biggest battle I ever had to tackle. Ask all my Family & Friends. They will tell you. Then again, they probably won't.

This fight has been mentally, physically and emotionally a force to be reckoned with. With God's grace and mercy, still I rise. By now you know it's my marriage. My middle school crush and high school sweetheart. Yes, all that and a bag of chips. Here lately nothing has been sweet. Just cycles on repeat. Now ain't that terrible? At the age of 49 years old, you would think that one should be living a blessed life, instead of a messed-up life. Especially when you're serving the Lord. Well, yes, I am, and I'm going to keep serving Him until I get it right. I'm just keeping it real. One thing is for certain and two things are for sure, God won't ever leave me nor forsake me.

I'm just amazed at how I'm just coming to grips that My God wants me to take this Giant down myself. With His Strength while standing on His Promises. His word tells me that I can do all things through Christ who strengthens me. Yes, I said it. I got all the tools to win and I'm not applying them to take down this Giant. "This one is yours, Nikki" I could hear the Holy Spirit just as clearly saying God gives you free will to make choices in life. God wants to see me overcome this Giant. I got it now, Holy Spirit. Use wisdom and prayer in everything. Wisdom and strength become your best friend in every situation. I could no longer focus on what others were doing. The moment I asked God to remove people and things out of my life, I began seeing my plate being cleaned off. I promise myself today that I will no longer allow people to pull on my love strings or my Christian walk. No more access. Goodbye to strongholds and toxic people. This fight must be fought with no feelings attached. Just wisdom and the strength of the Lord. I have so much power and wasn't even using it for the right battles.

Let's Pray: Lord, have Your way in the things I have no control over and give me strength and power to change the things I can change. I want to stand firm in this fight with peace and love in my heart. I pray that no bitterness comes with the decision that must be made. That no weapons would form from this fight. Show up mighty and strong for your daughter. May old things in my life be passed away so that new things can come forth. I pray for healing over my mind, body and spirit. In Jesus, holy name, it is done and all is well with you, Lord. Nothing but love from here on out. The fight is Over.

♫ **Song of the Day: Working for your Good by Kim Burrell**

Day 39

VIOLATION

Violation: the act of violating someone or something. A violation is an offense not a crime. I love to define the words that I use, even if I know the meaning of it. It is something about the definition of the word that I'm able to define myself or things I've been through in the words. This word could be used throughout my entire life. There were many times when I was violated by people, those that I thought loved me, family and so-called friends. They're the first ones that will do you wrong. But I'm fortunate enough to be able to know the true feeling of being violated and to learn to never inflict it on people that I love or just people in general. I'm not claiming to be perfect. All I ever wanted to be to others is a beacon of love.

The definition of violation isn't displayed violently enough for the things I witness in life. Yes, we all have our own interpretation of being violated. Small or big, being violated is just what it is. Nothing good comes out of it. No one should have to be treated that way. We all should be treating each other like we want to be treated. People will violate your privacy and your Heart for their own selfish gain. If you ever noticed, it's always the ones closest to you. Then, they'll try to declare their undying love for you. I'm not sure why I had to experience so many unhealthy traumatic experiences. I thought I was over the trauma in my life, but

I'm not. I still feel it as I bring them up today. I'm just able to deal with it a little differently with the Lord on my side.

Trauma isn't something that just goes away. It's an emotional response to horrible things that happen in our lives and the way to sustain it is too emotionally to detach from it. Trauma is an individual process. Everybody handles it in different ways. It will look different for each person. It's so funny I'm on this message. Prime example, I was working on this very page at 12:34pm on July 4, 2022. I kept telling my last two girls in the house to stop playing. They kept right on playing, ignoring what I had just said. I became mad at the fact that they violated the house rules. Of course there were other things leading up to it. Their rooms weren't cleaned. I felt like no one cared but me. They knew that there wasn't any fighting or horse playing in the house. Definitely not that time of night.

That night, I lost my cool and came out of character. They were used to seeing Godly girl but she wasn't there at that moment. I was now Nikki who would use choice words to get your undivided attention. Again, people can't just violate your space when it's a trigger point for you. Even if they do things to set off your trigger points, you as the individual must find other ways to surpass it. As small as it may sound, that very little thing is what triggered me. My middle girl, Kaz'jah came and tried to dissect the whole situation. I'm laughing now, because even though she's my child, in the end she was so right.

Let's talk about it. Talking about what triggers you sets boundaries for your loved ones. They'll know things to do and not do to set off your triggers. Abandonment was my childhood trauma. I didn't realize that being disregard was going to set me off. I'm just thankful for my kids. Even when I didn't know, God showed me the way, the truth and the light. The light was my children and our talk was my truth. Continue being aware and truthful. Face the fact that things happened in your life that may trigger points. Praying about it. This is how it's going to work for me now. Thanks to my two hard headed girls. You bring out the best in me.

Let us pray: Heavenly Father, thank You for each experience that happened in my life. Thank you for my shortcomings, my children and all of the things that I will endure in this life. You'll make a way for me to overcome abandonment issues and the trauma bond that happened at an early age. Father, thank You for allowing this situation to take place so that I could be more aware of it and know how to handle it from this day forward. I want to thank You because I know that You are showing me something in this devotional, and season of my life. I just want to thank You for keeping Your hands on me so that I may see the goodness in You in every situation in life. No matter what it looks like, I know that you are God. It is well. In Jesus' name , I pray. Amen.

♪ Song of the Day: Showing off by Sir the Baptist (Kierra Sheards)

Day 39

Dropping a Jewel

I know I told you early in the devotional about Dropping Jewels. I define Dropping Jewels as a connection between me and God. God downloads a word in me that I call jewels. Wherever I am in my mind-set, these are comforting thoughts and passages that I put down on paper and share with others.

Manifestation. What are you wanting for yourself? What are you praying for? What are you throwing into fertile ground? I believe it. I pray about it. Then, I wait to receive it. Sometimes, we don't realize that it's the things we say that sabotage our blessing. You must change your vocabulary. Change how you think. Get stronger in your prayer life. Every day you can manifest things. You can manifest your day by speaking life into it. I am everything God said I will be. Great things are happening for me because I believe it. In 2022, I believe in my heart that I'm going to travel the world to encourage, inspire and give hope to other women through my own personal experiences. The Women's Gathering will be a movement. I know for myself there's nothing too big or too hard for my God. I can have everything that God promises me. God is a way maker, a promise keeper and anything I need Him to be. I am free because of His grace & mercy. I am bold because He gives me the strength to be. I am blessed. My path is blessed. My walk is blessed. My family is blessed. My friends are blessed. Everyone that I come in contact with will be blessed. It's true . All you have to do is lift your hands and surrender to God. He'll bless you. Trust him. #TheGodlyGirl

Day 40

The Boat (Noah's Ark)

The Lord commanded Noah to build an ark in which his family and "every living thing of all flesh "(Genesis 6:19) were saved from the flood. Floodwaters destroyed the wicked and all the creatures that lived on the land except those in the Ark. When the flood water receded, Noah and his family exited the ark.

I'm not claiming to be Noah or anybody else for that matter but what I am saying is that I could connect with this story. As I began reading Noah's Ark, I started seeing pieces of me through the Women's Gathering. I kept reflecting on these visions. I could see myself out in the ocean, in these high waters, struggling to get to shore. I could see the silhouette of a Man on shore, but it never moved to assist me. I was sure he saw me. Why didn't he come to my rescue? I was doing all this struggling and there he was watching. I talked about this scenario happening to me for months. While in the ocean, I kept my eyes on this one bystander. I saw him sitting in a chair. Every time I had a vision, he was still there. Never coming to my rescue yet steadily watching me struggle. I went under a couple of times because of weariness from swimming. Though I went under, I always regained my posture and kept myself afloat.

This struggle went on for some years in my mind. Eventually, it started to reveal itself through my personal life. I couldn't figure out why I had to keep seeing this same vision. I saw people coming and going in and out of my life. I saw myself taking on other people's problems. I was fixing up everything but myself all while still in this ocean struggling. Not moving anywhere, just splashing water and wasting time. That's what it looked like. Just recently, I shared this with my God/sis Roxy. Her response was "Ummm, Nikki. You are a boat." "The Boat?" I said.

Yes, I was the boat. The boat that was going to help others to survive through their life experiences. After shedding a few tears and getting off the phone, I reflected on why it took me so long to receive this lesson. I had to quickly remind myself that it wasn't about the timing. It was about the fact that I did get it. Now, God is so amazing. I revisited that ocean scene a few more times and every time I would revisit it, I was still in the water with a different experience in my life. Everything around me was changing except for the situation of me being in the ocean and that bystander on shore. I remember getting frustrated because of what I was witnessing in the visions I kept seeing in my real-life situations. In real life, the cycles kept repeating and God kept showing me. I was struggling in real life. I was alone in real life. I was hurting and in denial in real life. No matter what God was showing me, I still wasn't getting it.

Even when you're in a situation, sometimes you must see it another way. The reason God wasn't allowing others to interfere was because He needed me to see things for myself. He wanted me to handle it on my own. Nobody was coming to rescue me. The longer I sat alone, I found Jesus. The more

I struggled, I began to trust Jesus. The more I read, the more I heard from the Holy Spirit. The Lord wanted me to find refuge in Him. He wanted me to see Him so everybody else had to go away.

This scenario or vision whatever you want to call it had to happen so I could know who to depend on (Jesus). He is not a man that He shall lie and this real-life experience had to happen so I could one day be able to share how God brought me out of situations, dark places, shame and abuse so I could be relatable to other people's experiences. This very experience was created to be a "Boat". A place where women can come, feel safe and be set free. I wouldn't have understood the "boat" message unless I had followed His plan.

Let us pray. Lord, I pray that for every woman reading this page and every woman that gets on this boat that You will have Your way. Touch their mind, body and spirit. May the Holy Spirit be invited into their lives, Lord. Give us strength to be what you called each of us to be, Father. Let your will be done. Let Healing take place so that our minds be made whole. Heal each of us from our head to our toes, Father God. Fill us with love, understanding, forgiveness and hope, Lord. May we believe in you so that our cups will run over with your word. In Jesus' Holy name, I pray. Amen.

♪ Song of the Day: Thank you Lord by Amber Bullock

Day 41

I Will Make You Hunger so When I bless, You'll be Humble.

I was looking for this verse somewhere in the Bible. I even Googled this entire sentence, "I will make you Hunger so when I bless You, you'll be humble" the way that I heard it. I was trying to figure out why the Holy Spirit said that to me. I was a little confused at the time because I was just getting to know God for myself. To be hearing from the Holy Spirit was an all time spiritual high. I will make you Hunger so when I bless you, you'll be Humble. That's all that kept playing in my little head. I didn't fully understand it until things around me started happening, One thing after another. For the life of me, I didn't understand why all these things were happening to me so fast. I just heard from the Holy Spirit and a few days later things were happening Suddenly. Every time something else would happen, I would return to that voice I heard. "I will make you hunger so when I bless you, you'll be humble."

One thing that I know to be true in this Christian walk is God will give you smoke signals before He'll give you the fire. Mother's Day week of 2019, things were looking up. I was in my new building working my business at The Spot Paint Studio. I received a call that was about to change my whole life. My trust in God was about to be tested from this phone call. Never in a million years would I have thought I would go from being blessed to now having less. Let's just call this situation "a test of faith". My child was in big trouble and I couldn't even see that she needed me until it was almost too late. All I kept saying was not my child, but yes it was my child and again I remembered hearing that voice that was so faint like a whisper. "I will make you hunger so when I bless you, you'll be humble."

I told myself you're about to go on a ride of a lifetime. I've always had my kids back. There was never a time that I wasn't going to be there for my kids. As long as I'm on this earth, I was always going to be by their side. That's a mother's mindset. Unfortunately, this situation was beyond my control. I asked God why this was happening again. Why was I going to have to hunger to be Humble? I wasn't a person that bragged. Only those people needed humbling experiences, not me. I was about to find out. Even though she was the one in trouble, it felt as though I was the one paying for it. Hurt, sickened, sleepless nights, crying, confused you name it. I didn't see it coming. Paying for lawyers and still trying to maintain my own finances. While doing my best not to go into that dark place because I had to be this strong woman for my kids. I felt like giving up and every time I spoke like that I heard the whisper. "No, you're not going to break. Just trust Me. Those were some powerful words and I was starting to believe it.

Every court appearance, I got hope. Every time we walked into the John Marshall Court Building, God's grace and mercy was with me and my family. It was definitely with my child. The more I went through this situation, the more God showed me Himself. I didn't even know what was really happening. I knew there was a situation that I thought was going to break me. Yet, the more I bent, the more God straightened things out. This wasn't my situation, but it was for me to go through it. it was for me to see the Goodness of God in even the darkest situations. You can't see in darkness. There's no hope in dark places. Only God could give me strength in this Matter. Every morning, noon and night, I was calling out to God. Every situation was building my relationship with Him.

The Moral to this story: It ain't none of what it looks like. God turned a major situation into no situation at all. It's a Must to know Him for yourself. Miracles, Signs and Wonders. I got to tell people about it. What He's done for me, He'll do the same for you. Believe him.

> Deuteronomy 8:3 "He humbled you, causing you to hunger and then feeding you with manna, which neither you nor your ancestors had known, to teach you that man does not live on bread alone but on every word that comes from the mouth of the Lord."

☀ Thought for Today:

You don't have to imagine what God will do in your life. Invite Him in so He can show you.

♪ Song of the Day: You're Going To See It Happen by: JJ Hairston

January 30, 2022

Omg! I woke up this morning still full of last night's event I hosted. The Women's Gathering Experience was the largest one I had so far. Lord willing, the next one will be even bigger. Waking up at 4 a.m. was a little too early to still be high off what I had experienced last night. I guess God wanted me in a prayer mood. For the last few months He's been waking me up at 3 and 4a.m. each morning to pray. So it was nothing different this morning. I did as I was told, prayed and fell back to sleep. I woke up at 7:30 a.m., enough time to get ready for church. When I tell you, I'm so thankful for pushing myself through the church doors. Every word my pastor spoke was the word that I needed. He was teaching us about Miracles, Signs and Wonders. The funny thing was that I spoke about it last at the Women's Gathering.

God sure has a way of showing Himself to me. I can't stop thinking about the event. There was so much love shown and given in one night. I met a lot of new people. The thing that stood out the most was realizing that there are a lot of women going through things in life. From self-esteem issues, childhood trauma, to loving the wrong people in life. You name it. We all have been through some things. I thank God for the outlet of freedom of the Women's Gathering Movement.

One day soon, you'll be speaking to millions at Women's Gatherings across the World, Nikki, Someone needs to hear your story to get through. Nikki Ross signing out at 12:15pm at Cracker Barrel.

Thank you for supporting a girl like me. I hope and pray that you enjoy every page in this devotional because life has taken me in many directions here lately. I'm just thankful that despite the many distractions, I stayed the course. I completed what some people close to me said I wouldn't. "Why do you always start something and never finish?" they would ask. I didn't take it personally because it was the truth. I'm always starting something. I'm just thankful for the loves who told me the truth about myself. Cheers to Kevin and Kaz'jah, because of you I finally finished something that I started. Thanks for your love and honesty. Cheers to a Women's Gathering Devotional 2022.

www.ingramcontent.com/pod-product-compliance
Lightning Source LLC
Chambersburg PA
CBHW071456160426
4319SCB000013B/2129